T4-AJZ-407

GOLDEN RULES FOR PARENTING
A Child Psychiatrist Discovers the Bible

by

Dan A. Myers, M.D.

Paulist Press
New York/Mahwah, N.J.

Scripture quotations are from *The Living Bible, Life Application Bible*, © 1988 by Tyndale House Publishers, Inc.

Cover design by Nighthawk Design

Interior design by Millennium Wordpress

Library of Congress Cataloging-in-Publication Data

Myers, Dan A., 1937-
     Golden rules for parenting : a child psychiatrist discovers the Bible / by Dan A. Myers.
          p.   cm.
     Includes bibliographical references.
     ISBN 0–8091–3777–1 (alk. paper)
     1. Child rearing—Religious aspects—Christianity.   2. Child rearing—Biblical teaching.   I. Title.
BV4529.M94   1998
248.´45—dc21   98–28246
                                                                              CIP

Published by Paulist Press
997 Macarthur Boulevard
Mahwah, New Jersey 07430

www.paulistpress.com

Printed and bound in the
United States of America

CONTENTS

To Simone, Yvette, Belén, Heather,
Lacy, Dan; and their children; and
their children's children

ACKNOWLEDGMENTS

Of the many wonderful people who contributed to my writing *Golden Rules for Parenting, A Child Psychiatrist Discovers the Bible,* the most inspirational to me, the person who made the greatest sacrifice, and my most demanding critic was my wife Kathy. Without her help and patience I could not have written this book.

Other family and friends who influenced my writing include:

My father, Rosy Myers, who instilled my strong respect for authority; and my mother, Jeri Myers, who all my life has made me feel as if I could succeed at anything.

My children, to whom the book is dedicated, and their spouses who read early drafts and made helpful suggestions.

Long-time friends, Dr. Bill and Sandra Snyder, who were particularly encouraging to me, as was the Highland Park Presbyterian Wednesday Morning Bible Study.

At various stages, others reviewed my work and gave helpful guidance. They include Dr. Moody and Freddie Alexander, Tom Amis, Jr., Dr. Clayton and Peggy Bell, Ron Cresswell, Jason Dupuy, Fritzi Dupuy, Dr. Irvin Ebaugh, Dr. David Green, Ron and Mary Macon, Dr. Bonham and Marcille Magness, Sue Main, Jane McKelvey, Dr. Jack and Ann Martin, Mary Jay and Peter Michel, Foster Poole, Lori Reinboldt, Nancy Seale, D.A. Sharpe, Anne Smith, Jenny and Mike Trant, Rev. Marshall Zieman, and a guardian angel disguised as my editorial consultant, Lucille Enix.

Introduction

One Sunday, while listening to a sermon, it occurred to me I had never read the biblical account of the life of Jesus Christ. The biblical depiction of Christ and his culture, unlike most biographies of ancient heroes, is not built on fragments of information pieced together years later. The biblical story of Jesus is a contemporaneous accounting by people who lived during his time and knew him well. Two authors of the gospels, Matthew and John, were disciples of Jesus. They spent twenty-four hours a day with him for three years. The author of the gospel of Luke was a Greek medical doctor who interviewed Jesus' mother, brothers, sisters, and disciples with the purpose of recording an accurate description of Christ's life and times. The gospel of Mark was written by John Mark, a companion to the apostles Peter and Paul. These descriptions by contemporaries of Jesus intrigued me. I read the New Testament, then the Old Testament, with an interest similar to reading an historical novel.

Reading the Bible cover to cover amazed me. For one thing, it was not as long as I had expected. I had the idea reading the Bible would be similar to reading an encyclopedia. The New Testament, which covers a hundred year time period, from the birth of Christ in 5 BC to the apostle John writing the book of Revelation in 95 AD, has only *323* pages.[1] By comparison, *Jurassic Park* by Michael Crichton is 399 pages. *The Firm* by John Grisham is 421 pages. The gospels, the first four books of the New Testament, tell about Jesus' life while on earth and focus on the gift of salvation and eternal life. There are only *146* pages, total, in the four books of the gospels.

The Old Testament is filled with drama and adventure, recounting *two thousand* years of history from Abraham to Christ. It tells how to please God, describing punishments for disobedience and rewards for obeying God's law. The Old Testament is *1,053* pages in length. That's long, but not much more than Larry McMurtry's book, *Lonesome Dove,* which is 945 pages.

The *entire* Bible is *1,373* pages, the same length as *Noble House* by James Clavell. Even though the Bible seemed shorter than expected, I was proud of myself when I completed reading it. I had personally known few people who had read the Bible "cover to cover." Of course most people don't brag about it. Also, I had not been associating with many people who gave reading the Bible a very high priority.

Perspective on this accomplishment came the day after I completed reading the Bible. While dropping off my dry cleaning I noticed that the manager, Samuel Kim, had an open Bible on the table. I told Mr. Kim I had just completed reading the entire Bible and could not resist asking him how much of it he had read. He modestly said he had read it for the twelfth time, *that year*! Mr. Kim had read the Bible 120 times. He said the first time he had opened a Bible, he read the New Testament through without sleeping. Although completing the Bible may not be as easy as reading a novel of the same length, Mr. Kim's example taught me humility, and that reading it *once* is not a superhuman feat.

As I read the Bible, I found child-rearing principles similar to those I use in my child psychiatry practice. Parenting advice, which I had assumed was modern or original, had been recorded in the Bible thousands of years ago. A friend, who knew of my new interest in the Bible, invited me to speak to his Sunday School class on "The Bible and Child-Rearing." That weekend my son was home from college so he attended the class. He listened as I explained how biblical teaching offers powerful guidance for parents raising children. After the lecture he said, "Dad, I am proud of you. I never knew you thought religion was important."

My son and three daughters, fourteen years earlier, had experienced the trauma of their mother and me ending a twenty-year marriage. It was a stressful time for us all. I coped by working excessively, running marathons, and drinking. My spiritual life was empty. The closest I ever came to church was when I jogged past one.

During that time, I learned that a college friend whom I had not seen in twenty years, Ann McFadden Lawson, was dying of cancer. The cancer had spread to her bones and she was suffering terribly. I was moved to call Ann, and to my surprise she said she had been thinking about calling me. Ann, a devout Christian, explained that she had been praying for her intractable pain to ease. However, she continued to suffer and wanted to know what psychiatry had to offer for pain management.

Ann was unable to leave her bed, so I met with her and her husband, Dr. Ray Lawson, at their home. We agreed that I would try hypnosis to relieve Ann's pain. Two to three times a week, until her death eighteen months later, Ann and I worked together. There seemed to be remarkable lessening of her pain; she was able to leave her bed and have a more active life.

During our sessions, Ann often discussed her feelings about having cancer, her impending death, the loss to her family, and the importance of her strong Christian faith. I would listen with empathy, struggling to find something to say that might be helpful to her. Thirteen years later, I began to appreciate the role Ann had played in directing me toward Christianity. When I wrote Ray to tell him of this realization, he responded, "Dan, you never knew it, but from the very first she was trying to help you."

When I married Kathy Hawn—who had two daughters, Heather and Lacy—their Christian family traditions immediately began to impact me. Dan Jr., my son, came to live with us, and soon, through Kathy's example and influence, we became a church-going family. Regular church attendance was enlightening and caused me to associate with other Christians.

My sister-in-law and her husband gave a *Life Application Living Bible* to me as a Christmas gift. Several months later, I opened the Bible to look up an historical point I had heard at a sermon. I was drawn to continue reading. One year later, I had read the Bible cover to cover and had begun writing this book.

Although reading the Bible and writing this book may have made me a better Christian, a better parent, and a better child psychiatrist, it has *not* made me a "Christian psychiatrist." I do not treat patients with religion. On the other hand, I have come to appreciate that living with *no* spiritual guidance handicaps families. Conveying to my children the good news of how the Bible can be used as a parenting manual was the motivation for this book.

CHAPTER ONE

The Bible as a
Child-Rearing Manual

Over 60,000 child interviews and thirty years of the study and practice of child and adolescent psychiatry have provided me with insights about parenting. These insights, in turn, have been tested repeatedly by my patients and their families. Still, deciding which information to include in a book on child-rearing was difficult. Ultimately, the Bible itself supplied direction. I began reading from Genesis, and I let the Bible lead me, stopping to write when a verse caused me to compare biblical teaching with my child psychiatric experience. For example, the chapter on honoring your father and mother is based on the ten commandments. The topics of child sexual behavior and child sexual abuse came to mind while reading the Bible's warnings about sexual immorality.

Everything written was, at least, provoked as I read the Bible. This resulted in significant issues not being included. One of my daughters mentioned that there was no chapter devoted to single parents. The guidelines in the Bible are applicable whether a parent is single or divorced. Also it seems consistent that the Bible, which emphasizes the importance of staying married, would leave out special instructions for helping those of us who divorce.

I concluded that using the Bible as a guide for writing a book on child-rearing should allow a safe course. Its teachings have been used to guide lives for 4,000 years. Child psychiatry has existed as a medical specialty only since 1957, and its theories are regularly being challenged and updated.

Although my writing may reflect my strengthening Christian beliefs, this book should also be useful for non-Christian parents. The book integrates, validates, and repudiates modern child-rearing practices by comparing them to parenting instructions found in the Holy Bible. Many of these biblical instructions are found in the Old Testament, common to both the Jewish and the Christian religions. Jesus was a Jew, and his devout parents reared him using Jewish child-rearing principles. My experience as a child psychiatrist convinces me that the directions for child-rearing given in the Bible are sound, regardless of one's religious beliefs.

None of the books in the Bible is devoted primarily to rearing children. There are instructions in the Bible for parents, but they are not grouped together conveniently in a particular book or chapter. Did God want us to have to look for them? Maybe they are scattered throughout scripture as an inducement to get us to read the entire Bible. I believe God is directing us to put childhood in perspective. Like the flight attendant who tells us to put the oxygen mask on ourselves before helping our children, God is telling parents to *first* make their own lives comply with his word, and then teach their children.

Jesus' Parents

During the time of Christ, angels sometimes spoke to humans. An angel (Luke 1:26 and Matthew 1:20) told Mary she would become pregnant, be conceived by the power of the Holy Spirit, and have a son whom she should name "Jesus." Angels (Luke 2:8–17) told shepherds that the Messiah was born in Bethlehem. In Matthew 2:13, an angel told Joseph to flee into Egypt to save Jesus from Herod, and an angel told him when it was safe to return to Israel (Matthew 2:19). Surprisingly, nowhere in the New Testament does it say God or his angels spoke to Mary and Joseph to give them child-rearing instruction for Jesus. Mary and Joseph must have possessed remarkable parenting abilities.

Matthew 1:1–17 traces Joseph's ancestry from Abraham through Isaac to Jacob to Judah, through King David, and King Solomon. Mary's lineage (Luke 3:23–38) runs back to Adam and Eve, through Noah, Abraham, and King David. Mary and Joseph shared a value system based on the word of God. They implemented their religious heritage in parenting Jesus. Their parenting instructions came from God through scripture. The same wisdom is accessible to parents today through reading the Old Testament. In addition, in the New Testament we have the benefit of the teachings of Jesus Christ.

Using the Bible in Modern Times

Neither the New nor Old Testament is written like a "How To" book on parenting. The Bible seldom gives instructions for specific life situations. Biblical directions are not rigid. Through the years, they have been applicable to other times and cultures. Neither the Bible, nor life, is always black or white.

Parents are regularly confronted by situations that come in shades of gray—for example, which television shows should be off-limits for children, and should restrictions be lifted as the children become more mature? If the parents' belief system includes moral standards as described throughout the Bible, countless judgments they will make on behalf of their children may be positively influenced.

It is not possible to completely screen children from all the immorality in our world. However, regular exposure of children to immorality does not better prepare them for adulthood. Their homes should be havens where they can grow and strengthen with a minimum of noxious influences. The more fixed children become in their value system, the better they can withstand an immoral world. A psychiatry professor explained it this way:

Suppose a man has a job where every day he is ridiculed and humiliated by his boss. Do you think that, to prepare him for work, his wife should hit, curse, and snub him at home? No, he needs respite from the cruelty and harshness. The confusion and immorality we too often see in our world does not mean that protecting our children through biblical direction is irrelevant; rather, it causes us to need the Bible more!

Modern discoveries about human development and behavior can help in understanding a child and can provide guidance or treatment when problems occur. For example, counseling for parents in marital turmoil may prevent a divorce. Recognizing a child's learning disability and providing remedial teaching and schooling can expand his or her educational potential. The diagnosis and treatment of attention deficit disorder, depression, drug abuse, obsessive compulsive disorder, and other disorders during childhood not only result in better adjusted children, but treatment may also prevent mental illness when they become adults. Suicidal adolescents and children can be identified, protected, and successfully treated. Out-of-control children and teenagers may be hospitalized to interrupt dangerous, self-destructive behavior.

When psychiatric theories and treatment are supported by scripture, this increases our confidence in applying them. Does this mean the theories not found in the Bible should be discarded? Not necessarily. The Bible does not mention insulin, antibiotics, or chemotherapy, yet we use them feeling no conflict with biblical teaching. A proper perspective would be for parents to be cautious about accepting an explanation, recommendation, or treatment for their child if it *contradicts* biblical teaching. Examples might be a therapist's recommendation to divorce, live with a lover, or ignore parents' rules or the Bible's direction.

Most psychiatrists have been trained not to intrude into their patients' religious lives. Unfortunately, when the psychiatrist whom the patient trusts and respects does not even mention religion, the patient may assume the psychiatrist sees religious convictions as having no value. This may inadvertently cause the patient to ignore or abandon religious beliefs for psychological theories proposed by the therapist. Ironically, the psychiatrist may be relying on religious guidelines for the good mental health of his or her own family. When someone needs treatment for emotional problems, it might be ideal to use a devout and scholarly clergyman, also trained as a psychiatrist. However, the time-consuming training required for both professions makes this impractical. It appears the best option is to put your faith in the word of God and then seek professional assistance.

Whether a child safely navigates the dangers of growing up is determined by many factors. Some children seem born more flexible, resilient, and adaptable than others. Although our interaction with our children can modify their behavior, sometimes the outcome may be largely pre-determined by their genetic makeup.

CHAPTER TWO

The Genes in the Jeans

Whether nature (heredity) or nurture (environment) determines personality has been debated for centuries. Some people strongly believe that environment, will-power, and effort shape what we become. Others feel our ancestors' genes have set our life course. There is a religious analogy to this argument. Some Christians strongly believe God gives us free choice. Others emphasize that God has our life already planned or predestined. Most scientists conclude both heredity and environment shape us. Most theologians agree God does have a plan for our lives, but also permits some free will. These questions have practical implications for parents when they set standards for their children. The difficulty comes in distinguishing what can be changed and what cannot.

What can parents expect from a child? What fundamental strengths has he or she been born with? Do children have weaknesses that cannot be overcome? Which of their characteristics have been inherited, which have been learned, and which have been shaped by their environment? The answers to these questions may be the keys to opening doors for a child's success.

Adoption

One interesting way to compare heredity with environment is by studying identical twins who have been adopted into different homes. It is remarkable to see how personality traits and behavioral patterns of twins remain similar despite growing up in very different environments. The results of such studies are fascinating and leave no doubt that heredity plays a major role in whom we become. However, the conclusions have limited value for an *individual* parent. Predicting height, build, intelligence, artistic ability, and physical coordination may be statistically relevant, but is not one hundred percent valid. A particular child may not fit the pattern exhibited by the other ninety-nine. Neither do statistics give credit for the strength of the human will, nor the power of prayer.

Parents whose children are "natural" could learn from parents who adopt. Although most adults prefer to have children from their own genetic pool, adopting can be enriching for parents, and bring about inconceivable opportunities and happiness for the child.

Adopting a child can be a loving and selfless act. Some parents deliberately adopt emotionally damaged, physically limited, or intellectually inferior children to give them a healing home and family life. These parents seem to exemplify God's love, just as he adopted us knowing our faults, sinful nature, and weaknesses. St. Paul writes in Galatians 4:5–7 and Ephesians 1:5 of how we have been "adopted" into God's family by Christ's dying for us. We have become his very own children, and may speak of God as "Father." Many parents accept their adoptive children as God created them, seeing themselves as nurturers to guide children to their full potential. They do not try to make their child into what they "wish" he or she could be. Most adopting parents work to discover their child's innate abilities, since they know their child does not share their genetic makeup. However, when parents adopt children and then *deny* the significance of the children's heredity, the results can be most unfortunate.

It is not possible for children to be something they are not. Children will sense it if they are a disappointment to their parents. When children get older, dissatisfaction and conflict can become more overt. Such conflict may culminate when a child becomes a teenager. An unhappy adopted child may abandon the effort of working out his or her problems for the fantasy that "things would have been different if I had my real parents." Parents of a depressed, angry, impulsive, defiant teenager may also want to deny that the child is their responsibility. When the child is adopted, it makes this denial more plausible. I have known parents who attempted to return their adopted child to the state after he or she has become a difficult teenager. Other parents, feeling they have been burdened with an unsatisfactory child, sued their adoption agency. If it were possible, some natural parents might take similar action.

Such scenarios are rare. Most parents find raising an adopted child to be as satisfying and fulfilling as having a natural child. Many households are made up of a gratifying mix of adopted and natural children. Raising an adopted child should require no different methods than those used with "natural" children. However, it is important for adoptive parents to recognize their child will be less like them than if he or she was "natural." Personality traits, as well as specific physical characteristics, often can be traced through many generations. Behaviors may be learned or taught, but temperament and some personality traits are inherited. Loving and emotionally strong parents may be able to modify and redirect an adopted child's personality, but it may be more of a struggle than the parents anticipated.

The foregoing discussion reminds adopting parents there will be things about their child that they cannot change. The child, to some degree, will come with his or her own pre-programmed, pre-destined direction. Most adopting parents already know this. *Natural* parents may be not as aware that they can face the same issue. Chance, or divine planning, determines which genes we receive. I have seen children who, because of heredity, remain incorrigible despite dedicated, skillful, loving parents. There are families where a natural child has psychiatric problems, while the adopted brother or sister is high-achieving and emotionally stable. There is no way to foresee which of the millions of genetic combinations for physical and personality traits a *particular* child will receive. Each child born to natural parents has a statistical chance of being as unfamiliar and different as a child who is adopted. Parents are sometimes heard to say as they observe behaviors of their child, "Where did he or she come from?" Natural parents have a greater tendency to *assume* their child is like them, and are more prone to misgauge their child's innate strengths and/or weaknesses. Natural parents will be misled if they expect a son or daughter, who may physically resemble a natural parent, to have that parent's intelligence, temperament, interests, and skills. Parents should evaluate their *natural* children with discernment and objectivity as if the children were adopted. Some children just *seem* to be more like us than others.

Raising Children Who Are Not Like Us

Children born with personality characteristics such as aggressiveness, unresponsiveness to affection, learning differences, moodiness, or sleeplessness will be particularly challenging for parents who come from families where these traits are foreign. There are no jokes about inheriting a grandmother's rigidity, an uncle's hyperactivity, or an aunt's temper. Instead, the parents may become frustrated by the unfamiliarity of the child's response.

For example, parents might bring their child for psychiatric evaluation because of bed wetting, possibly inherited from an unknown relative. Other parents, who themselves were bed wetters, may wait patiently for their child to "grow out of it." Parents who are rigid, compulsive, and serious may have great difficulty with a child who is disorganized, impulsive, and volatile. In a different family this child's personality traits might be the norm and perceived as desirable.

Inherited physical, personality, and intellectual characteristics of a child hold different importance to some families compared to others. Parents who have satisfying jobs that require no college degree might be more accepting of a child with a learning difference than parents who are college professors. Intellectually gifted, but physically uncoordinated, children could be more appreciated in academic families than they would be by parents greatly interested in athletics. Children's inborn strengths and weaknesses will drive the direction of their personalities, but these inborn traits will be accepted, rewarded, or criticized depending on the personalities and value systems of the parents. The parents' *reaction* to a child will greatly influence the child's self-image, self-esteem, and self-confidence.

How parents manage their children will shape the children's behavior and how they adjust to society. A nine-year-old boy, Scott, since being a toddler, has been cautious, careful with his toys, and responsive to his parents' commands. His eight-year-old sister, Samantha, is impulsive, careless with her possessions, and must be told repeatedly before she obeys. The parents tell Scott and Samantha to clean up their rooms. Scott goes directly to his room and restores whatever is awry to its regular place. Samantha initially ignores the request, then argues she is too busy, and begins to cry, saying Scott messed up her room.

The parents recognize they will never change Samantha to be like Scott. However, Samantha *still* must clean her room; this means it will take effort by her parents to see that she does it. In the process, and through thousands of similar battles, Samantha will learn to respect authority, to control her impulsiveness, and to appreciate the disadvantages of being disorganized and careless. Forcing Samantha to clean her room creates an uproar for the family. In the short run, it would be easier to accept Samantha as "not being born to do housework."

Samantha, on the other hand, is always eager to play outside with her friends, enjoys sports, and excels in athletics. Scott prefers to be inside, to watch TV and play video games. Scott tends to be overweight, and the parents have to push him to exercise or be involved with peers. The parents realize Scott is different from Samantha, but this does not mean they should accept Scott as "being born to be a hermit."

Parents, depending on their own heritage and upbringing, may have more difficulty with a child like Samantha than like Scott, or vice versa. This, of course, is no justification for avoiding confronting a child's behavior. In the final analysis, the *parents* make the difference whether children use inborn abilities to their best advantage. *Parents,* recognizing their children's frailties, must decide when to assist their children to avoid a problem, or when to push them to overcome a weakness, permitting them to sink or swim. Such determinations come easily and naturally *if* you know your child. Parents are excellent judges of their children's ability *if* they spend time observing and interacting with them. Family life can modify a child's inheritance, but the "genes in the jeans" exert a powerful force.

Modifying the Serenity Prayer used in Alcoholics Anonymous makes it very applicable for parents: "God, give me *time* with my children so I *understand* them, give me the *strength* to change those things about them I should, the *patience* to accept those things I cannot change, and the *wisdom* to know the difference." Successful parents will "know the difference" early in their child's life. The first five years for the child are crucial.

CHAPTER THREE

The Important First Five Years

It might have been logical for Jesus to come to earth as a powerful adult who would rescue the Jews from their enemies. Jesus' arrival as a baby and his being raised like other human children made his acceptance as a Messiah much more difficult. God must think having a childhood is important; why else would he have sent the Messiah, his Son Jesus Christ, to earth as an *infant*?

Child psychiatrists identify the first five years of a child's life as crucial for building the foundation on which much of adult personality is created. Parents have great responsibility and opportunity during their child's early years. Childhood is a time when parents have the most potential for influencing the course of their children's lives. Parents never again will have such power and control. Parents receive more of their children's love, respect, and attention when their children are young. What a tragedy when parents do not shape their children during this crucial stage, or use this opportunity only to "entertain" them.

Child-rearing does not require parents to *give up* eighteen years of their lives for their children. To the contrary, this is not good for a child. Raising children does *not* last a lifetime. It is a time-limited joy and responsibility. Assuming children leave home at eighteen, they will have spent twenty-two percent of their lives under some influence of their parents. Conversely, *seventy-eight percent* of a parent's life will *not* involve child-rearing. Parenting is relatively short. It behooves us to use this time advantageously.

The Parenting Race

Parenting can be compared to running a race. In a race, maximum effort is needed at the beginning. If a runner doesn't get off to a good start, he or she may never make up for lost time. If the runner does get off to a good start, the remainder of the race will go smoothly unless unforeseen complications arise. An unnoticed pothole causing a fall, an untied shoe, being bumped or tripped by another runner, muscle cramps, and other unexpected happenings can threaten a performance. In a recent race, a train blocked the course. The race director opened both doors of a boxcar and the runners passed through it. When the unexpected happens, a successful runner will make adjustments, intensify his or her efforts, and soon return to his or her stride.

The Important First Five Years

For parents, the start of the race begins with their child's first five years of life. At the child's "start," parents need to devote their most concentrated effort. A bad start can cause parent and child never to get into a comfortable pace. Struggling to overcome a child's unsuccessful and unhappy first five years of life is difficult and often painful. There is no opportunity to start over again. Ready or not, this race will proceed.

With a good first five years, the final thirteen years the child will have at home should go smoothly unless unexpected complications arise. Problems such as divorce, physical illness, financial misfortune, disruptive moves to other cities, drug abuse, or other unforeseen crises sometimes happen. When these occur, successful parents make adjustments. They shift back into a sprint, increasing their time and effort with their children. With perseverance, prayer, and sometimes professional assistance, parents should be able to resume a more comfortable pace toward the finish.

The race of parenting has an unusual twist. At the finish line of eighteen years, the child whom you had been coaching will pull away from you and begin his or her own sprint. To your surprise, you will realize *your* race is not over. You still have one-half of life's course to run. Parenting a child is a fairly short segment in the race of life. Is it too much to expect parents to devote enough time and energy to do it right?

Parents will ask: But how do we do it right? Some answers will be found throughout this book. However, appreciating the importance of childhood, and staying in the race, themselves may be enough. Some parents never teach or show their child how to run. Other parents are unfocused, distracted, or unavailable when their child falls and needs a helping hand. Parents who fail with their children today often know what to do; they just don't do it. Do you think that parents don't know their children would be better off if the family went to church? Parents *know* violent and sexually explicit TV and movies are not good for their children. Some parents have other priorities and, either at the start, during the sprint, or along the straightaway, may decide they "just don't like track." Unfortunately, it is the child who becomes the loser.

Writing directions for parenting can make it sound more complicated than it really is. Consider writing instructions for catching a baseball. Can you imagine the complexity of programming a computer to calculate the changing velocity, altitude, and direction of a fly ball? Specific written instructions for parenting can be equally intimidating. Children have a natural tendency to grow up healthy if they are protected and receive adequate guidance and nurture. Parents who have had a fairly normal childhood themselves (particularly if raised with religious influence), and who love their child, and devote time to their family, will *automatically* do most things right.

Stages of Development

The parenting process is difficult to describe because there are so many factors, and these factors are continually changing. Parenting attitudes and methods that are appropriate at one time in a child's life may be harmful at a later stage. A child's personality emerges through a process that child psychiatrists know as "developmental lines." This concept describes how the child's personality passes through one stage, followed by another, usually in an orderly and predictable manner. For example, children crawl before they walk, and walk before they are able to run. An infant first coos, garbles, says words, then sentences, followed by the stepwise development of fluid speech.

Emotional growth proceeds in a similar fashion. Infants first bond to their mother (the symbiotic or oral stage), then learn they are separate and have their individual identities (separation-individuation stage), then establish a degree of independence from their mother and exert self-control (anal stage). By approximately five years of age, children have resolved inter-psychic conflict about giving up their attachment to their parents and proceed into the latency phase where energy is primarily devoted to making friends and learning in school. Following latency, adolescence begins with its own step-by-step developmental process.

Disruption of one of these stages may affect the child's passage through stages of development yet to come. Psychiatrists believe traumatic events that adversely affect the child's development are the source of many mental disorders of childhood and adult life. The earlier in a child's life that a psychological trauma occurs, the greater the likelihood it will have a significant impact on other stages.

Traumatic events, such as a mother's death in early childhood, can have far-reaching consequences to a child's mental health and emotional stability. For example, a child develops "basic trust" early in life. The death of the mother could cause a defect in the infant's ability to trust others and thus would influence every stage through which the child passes. Such a severe early trauma to the child could have great impact on that child's adult personality. Deficiency in the "basic trust" area could limit and influence the qualities of all future relationships.

Of course there are many other factors that influence whether mental illness or mental health results. These include the severity of the psychological stress and the basic ego strengths of the child. Ego strengths can be thought of as the assets with which the child is born— such attributes as physical health and stamina, temperament, resilience, flexibility, and intelligence.

Successfully completing each developmental step opens up unlimited possibilities for the next stage. It is this feature that causes the practice of child psychiatry to be so rewarding. Removing even a small block in a child's early life can have great impact. If through psychiatric treatment hyperactive, angry, depressed, fearful, or anxious children become able to participate in usual childhood activities, it will allow them countless opportunities for emotional growth that otherwise would have remained blocked. Helping a child so he or she can attend scouts, play sports on a team, be in a class play, or try out to be a cheerleader allows him or her to make friends. What a different course a young child's life might have taken had he or she remained in a hyperactive, angry, depressed, home-bound, and friendless state.

Parents must adjust their methods as a child matures.

In the first two years of a child's life there should be an emphasis on protecting and nurturing. The infant must feel secure and loved. Into the "terrible twos" and through age five, the children need to learn self-control, to honor their father and mother, to develop respect for authority, to have a sense of sexual identity, and to relate to other children in a give-and-take manner. During grade school, children focus on academic learning, developing self-discipline, enjoying competition, playing by rules, and beginning social relationships outside the family. In adolescence, parents *must protect* their teenagers whose judgment may be faulty, but not prevent them from becoming more independent. When it is not too dangerous, and when the consequences are not grave, children need to learn from experience. It takes involved and discerning parents to judge if a particular experience offers greater opportunity for growth or harm to their children.

Parents will make millions of decisions affecting their children's lives. Fortunately a *few hundred* misguided parental actions usually do not counteract *all* the positive decisions parents make in their child's behalf. Often I console parents who feel they have mishandled a particular conflict with their child by reminding them they will have *many* other opportunities to make their point.

Parents should keep in mind that the goal of raising children is to assist them to become self-sufficient enough to safely *leave* home. Children are a gift *on loan* from God. Parents lose perspective when they raise children as *their* unique possessions. Parents' feeling of self-worth can become dependent on their children's achievements. A child can become the center of the parents' world. The Bible has an answer for the question, "Which came first, the chicken or the egg?" in Genesis 2:7, "And the Lord God formed man of the dust of the ground, and breathed into his nostrils the breath of life; and man became a living soul." God made Eve from Adam's rib, and later Eve gave birth to Cain (Genesis 4:1). The "chicken" came first. God did not start the human race by creating a child. Some parents respond to their child as if he or she were the center of the universe. God's first commandment (Exodus 20:3) says we should put no other gods before him. That would include idolizing a child.

Child Worship

In my practice of child psychiatry, I have seen parents who appear to worship a child. Typically, this is an only child born late in the parents' lives. The parents may refer to the child as "their little miracle." There is an interesting analogy in the Bible. Four thousand years ago (Genesis 21:1–5) Sarah, who was ninety years old, and Abraham, who was one hundred years old, had their first son, Isaac. In their case, their "little miracle" really was a miracle. Imagine the amount of "doting" that must have occurred from these one hundred-year-old parents. Their adoration of baby Isaac may have been close to "worship."

It was horrifying to me to read that God commanded Abraham to kill Isaac as a sacrifice (Genesis 22:2) to test Abraham's love for God. The Bible does not say Isaac was selected for sacrifice because Sarah and Abraham had such intense love for their son that it had become a form of worship. However, I speculate God may have used this example to remind us of the danger of putting a child before God. When Abraham demonstrated his willingness to obey God and sacrifice his son, Isaac was spared (Genesis 22:12). In the ten commandments (Exodus 20:15) God describes himself as "jealous," punishing the children as well as the parent for a parent's idolatry. Although parents' joy and love for a newborn may be immense, it must have bounds. From a biblical perspective, and also from a child psychiatric position, worshiping your child can lead to disaster.

Parents who idolize their children will "jump" when the children command. Children who grow up in an environment where every whim is quickly satisfied may not only fail to develop the character to be successful adults, they may become tyrants or feel like gods. Reality sets in when parents are no longer able to sustain a child's "personal heaven." This can happen when children enter pre-school or as late as high school graduation, if parents are exceptionally adept at shielding children from the consequences of their behavior. Teenagers may flagrantly break traffic rules when they know their parents can and will keep them from being prosecuted. Rude and obnoxious behavior to teachers may continue if parents use enough power to squash a teacher's attempt at discipline. A teenager throws paint over her ex-boyfriend's car, knowing her parents will pay to have it repainted. One teenage boy, who was angry with his girlfriend, drove a truck with oversize tires over the top of her car, knowing his parents would take care of the repairs. When children eventually find, to their great rage and despair, that the rest of the world no longer recognizes their "god-like" powers, they may have *huge* "temper tantrums." Parents may discover that the "heaven" they created during childhood later turns into the "hell" of raising an out-of-control adolescent.

Frustration at not having their needs continually met can cause such rage in children that they commit violence against themselves or others. Suicide is a leading cause of death in teenagers, surpassed only by accidents and homicide. According to the Bible (Genesis 2:8), the first murder was committed by Cain, the first-born of Adam and Eve's children, when he killed his brother Abel. Although some children seem to be "born bad," I believe it is fair to speculate this was not true of Cain. Adam and Eve, freshly created by God, would not have been carrying genes from unstable, violent relatives. Cain had been raised as if he was the only child on earth, and, as a matter of fact, he *was* the only child on earth. He may have been unable to tolerate the loss of attention when his brother Abel was born.

In the Old Testament, murder of a sibling occurred with some frequency. Cain killed Abel (Genesis 4:8), Esau plotted to kill Jacob (Genesis 27:41), Joseph's brothers tried to kill him (Genesis 37:18–24), Solomon (1 Kings 2:25) had his brother, Adonijah, killed. I have evaluated two children who killed their siblings. One was a thirteen-year-old boy who killed his ten-year-old half-brother whom he thought received preferential treatment from his parents. The other was a sixteen-year-old girl who killed her nineteen-year-old brother for taunting her. Thankfully, over-indulgence of a child does not regularly lead to murder. However, psychiatrists often see patients who carry a lifelong hatred toward a sibling whose birth forced them out of an "Eden" created by their parents.

It would be interesting to know more about Jesus' childhood. The Bible suggests he was raised like most other children. The people in his hometown of Nazareth remembered him as being like everyone else. When Jesus returned to preach in Nazareth (Matthew 13:55), the people said, "How is this possible? He is just a carpenter's son, and we know his mother and his brothers, James, Joseph, Simon, Judas, and his sisters." It appears that *even* the Messiah was not raised like a Messiah.

The challenge is for parents to give children the considerable attention they need during childhood without causing them to feel entitled, or to rob them of the opportunity to deal with adversity and develop strength of character. This task is complicated by children being in a continuous process of physical, intellectual, and emotional change and growth. Parents' reactions to a child's particular behavior will need to vary depending on the child's intellectual and emotional maturity. The younger the child, the more the parents will need to protect him or her from the outside world.

Nothing during childhood is more crucial for children than their parents' love and the love of God. Young children experience God's love through their relationship with their parents. Parents are messengers for God's love.

CHAPTER FOUR

Parents—Messengers for God's Love

The most damaging of all parents are those who give their children *no* love. Psychiatrists are quick to recognize the importance of love for a child. Scientific writings, such as those of Bowlby,[1] Harlow,[2] and Spitz,[3] attest to the danger of unavailable, insufficient, or inadequate parental love. Without love and attention, an infant may become retarded or die. Through the loving, protective relationship of parents, a child learns "basic trust" and develops "self-esteem." Sigmund Freud's equivalent of love, "libido," is said to be the fundamental drive that shapes all personal relationships.

The message of God's love pervades the Bible. The Old Testament repeatedly depicts God's love as he commands, guides, reprimands, and forgives his chosen people. The New Testament stresses the love of God, shown by the sacrifice of his Son for our sins. John 3:16 clearly explains this love: "For God so loved the world that he gave his only Son that whosoever believes in him shall not perish but shall have everlasting life." Paul said in 1 Corinthians 13:13, "There are three things that remain—faith, hope, and love—and the greatest of these is love."

Parents have a responsibility to teach their children of God's love (Deuteronomy 6:7; Psalm 22:30). However, very young children have difficulty grasping the concept of God. They look to parents for love and protection. Parents, not God, hold and soothe them. Parents, not God, hug and kiss them. Parents, not God, tell them they are loved. Parents, not God, look under the bed and in the closet to assure them when they are frightened. Parents, not God, clothe and feed them. Young children experience God's love through their parents. Parents are *messengers* for God's love.

To be an effective messenger, there is an unequivocal condition: you must have a *message!* If parents don't know what God's love is like, they will either convey it inaccurately or make up their own personalized version. What a mess this could, *or has,* become. In John 15:12, Jesus commanded us to love one another as he loves us. The Bible is the place to learn how God loves us.

Some parents overvalue the impact of *telling* their children they love them, minimizing that God's love also includes *protecting, teaching, disciplining,* and *punishing.* For example, Moses and David, both greatly loved by

God, were severely punished for their transgressions. Moses was denied access to the promised land because he did not fully obey an instruction from God (Numbers 20:7–12). David's son was taken from him and Bathsheba as punishment for their adultery (2 Samuel 12:13–18).

Unconditional Love

Although the Old Testament repeatedly demonstrates God's love and forgiveness, and the New Testament says that God's love is not earned but given, neither called God's love "unconditional." In Luke 15:11–31, Jesus describes a parent who welcomes the return of his wayward son. Although sometimes quoted as an example of God's unconditional love, to me it seems a better example of God's capacity to forgive. I suspect the father's reception for the prodigal son would not have been as warm if the son had not asked forgiveness and renounced his former lifestyle.

I discussed this concept of unconditional love with several ministers and friends. One minister said she felt "unrelenting" was more accurate than "unconditional" in describing God's love. Others felt that I was implying salvation depended on "works" rather than "grace." This was not the intent and is contrary to my beliefs. However, as a model for loving children, the "unconditional" aspect of God's love is *not* the primary feature. From my clinical experience, overemphasis of unconditional love can be unhealthy for children.

Children who are bathed in unconditional acceptance may be deprived of opportunities for overcoming or compensating for weaknesses. It is hard for a child to develop competence and character when parents continually arrange the child's life to make difficulties and hardships be resolved without effort. Although it is destructive for children to experience chronic failure and loss of hope, it is also damaging to "love" their frailties away by *over*protecting them from adversity. Some children develop outstanding study habits as they struggle to compensate for a learning disorder. On the other hand, some students give up immediately if an academic task requires effort, because they have grown accustomed to being allowed to bypass difficult work. In Romans 5:3–4, Paul says we should rejoice in our trials and problems since they are good for us and build strength of character. This does not mean that parents should not help their children. Parents can assist and encourage children to attempt tasks that will blossom into satisfying accomplishments. Parents, by supporting and praising their children's positive behavior, can promote self-esteem based on reality and competence.

Children who don't experience consequences will not modify their behaviors. These children will appear "immature," being late to learn lessons their peers learned in childhood. They give up easily and may underachieve academically, athletically, and interpersonally. Slight failure or reprimand is interpreted as being "not loved." Children who are indulged and rewarded, regardless of their behavior, become bewildered, frustrated, and enraged when the outside world does not love or even tolerate them unconditionally. Continually feeling that they are unjustly rejected or persecuted makes them at risk for drug use, depression, and suicide.

Self-Esteem

Parents may use unconditional love as a method for building their child's "self-esteem." Maintaining children's self-esteem by meeting their every need, wish, and demand will cause them to be spoiled, demanding, selfish, and inconsiderate of others. Children with these unappealing qualities are limited in the pleasure they can bring to others and to themselves. The quest for self-esteem can cause parents and child to disregard reality. For example, a boy develops the misconception that he is an excellent baseball player when, in reality, his "esteem" is built by his father buying baseball uniforms for the team, coaching, and maintaining his son in a role (usually pitcher) that exaggerates the child's actual ability. Such distortions cannot be maintained forever. Eventually the boy will be faced with the painful reality that his skills are less than he was led to believe. Parents may expand their children's social life by providing increasingly expensive toys, birthday parties, or trips that will attract "friends" and make the children "popular." These children may avoid learning the "give and take" of interpersonal relationships, relying on their parents to provide friends. When this contrived popularity can no longer be sustained, the children are hurt.

Such practices rob the children of opportunities to develop other "real" strengths they possesses. For example, it would be unfortunate if a girl never developed her genuine talent for piano, tennis, golf, or karate because her parents continued to promote her as a ballet dancer. Likewise, a boy's artistic talents could lie dormant while his father pushes him to play football.

Many parents and children measure their self-worth by worldly rather than heavenly standards. We fret, worry, and badger our children to be popular and admired. Our criteria for measuring our children's successes are fickle. What is "in" today becomes "uncool" tomorrow. What a frustrating and unrewarding task for a child to chase such changing, and often unrealistic, ideals. What a weight would be taken off their shoulders if children believed that God, not popular opinion, was their judge. It is not always easy to live a life that is pleasing to God, but we all come with the tools to accomplish it. We don't have to be pretty, smart, strong, agile, clever, or rich. Wouldn't it make a difference if our children realized this? Wouldn't it be a relief? Wouldn't they feel more self-confident? Couldn't this be their basis for self-esteem? It is so much more reasonable and fulfilling to teach our children the clear and lasting criteria that the Bible suggests for pleasing God.

"Self-esteem" is the buzzword of the 1990s. School counselors, teachers, mental health workers, psychologists, and psychiatrists preach to parents the importance of a child having good self-esteem. Books, magazines, and newspaper articles pertaining to child development list techniques and methods for assuring your child has self-esteem. Government programs instruct schools in how to raise a child's self-esteem. Self-esteem *is* important for a child. However, it should be an esteem steeped in the child developing true competence, not a phony sense of "I am a wonderful person because I am." In Romans 12:3 Paul says, "As God's messenger I give each of you God's warning: be honest in your estimate of yourself."

There is *no* place in the Bible where parents are told to try to develop self-esteem in their children. God is not described trying to develop self-esteem in the people of Israel. To the contrary, the Bible devotes considerable time instructing us of the dangers of over-valuing our importance. God repeatedly punished his people when they became puffed up with too much self-esteem. Luke 18:14 quotes Jesus as saying, "For the proud shall be humbled, but the humble shall be honored." If there is a reference to self-esteem in the Bible, it is in the context of being secure and unafraid because we are created in the image of God (Genesis 1:27). In Matthew 10:29 Jesus tells us if God watches over the sparrows in the sky, then he certainly will care for us. This belief that children are of unique value because of the love of God is very different from the self-esteem manufactured by many of today's parents. It is the emphasis on the "self" and the neglect of the importance of the love of God that corrupts the self-esteem principle.

God's Love

It seems odd that love *from God* is so seldom mentioned by parents to their children. Children feel protected, secure, and comforted when they are told God loves them. Children delight in singing, "Yes, Jesus loves me, the Bible tells me so." How many of us strive for our children to *first* live their lives to please God? Do we show our children we have high regard for them when they obey the word of God and practice the teachings of the Bible? How well do we convey the hope for their future if they are loved by God? Don't conceal this magnificent gift from your children.

Teaching children they are loved by God also helps *parents.* It can be a staggering and dangerous responsibility if parents become a "god" for their children. Even if parents have immense affection and dedication to child-raising, they are sometimes not loving. Accepting God's love for children relieves parents of the impossible task of being perfect. When parents assume responsibility for providing *all* of a child's love, it leaves the child uniquely vulnerable to loss. Parents may be separated from their children by divorce, illness, or death. What a comfort for children *and* parents to know that whatever happens, God will always be there for them. God's love is omnipresent.

Jesus says in Luke 9:48, "Anyone who takes care of a little child like this is caring for me." In Matthew 19:14–15 he says, "Let the little children come to me. For such is the Kingdom of Heaven." Then he put his hands on their heads and he blessed them. Children who grow up knowing they are loved by God should be secure, confident, and unafraid. Parents, *God's messengers,* must deliver this hopeful lesson. When parents are carrying the message of God's love, they are spending *quality* time with their children.

CHAPTER FIVE

What Is "Quality Time"?

Most of the time that parents spend with children can be "quality time." It will include fun times, difficult times, and dull times. Parents have a tendency to see "quality time" as only when parent and child share a special experience that leaves parents with a warm feeling of unique camaraderie or friendship. Examples I have heard include watching a son land a big bass, a mother helping her daughter into her first party dress, and having a family picnic or vacation. Those are memorable times, but stockpiling these elusive "quality times" is not the crux of being a loving and effective parent. Instead, they are the frosting on the cake, the strokes we need to encourage us to continue the *work* of parenting when we might otherwise tire.

"Quality time" is when parents are implementing the

message of God's love described in the previous chapter. Jesus Christ's relationship with his disciples, whom he referred to as "children," is an excellent model for what "quality time" can be: Jesus *spent time* with, and was an *example* for, his children. Jesus *protected* his disciples, but *prepared* them to *go out on their own*. Jesus *sacrificed* for his children and *taught them* how to *receive the gift of immortal life*.

Spend Time with Your Children

Once Jesus began his ministry, he lived night and day with his disciples. Jesus *spent time* with his "children." At today's hectic pace, often with both parents working, parents may have *limited* time with their children. Parents frequently ask how they can be more effective with their child-time, how they can make it "quality time." In responding to their question, I must be careful not to support a notion that the *total* time spent with their children is less important. No matter how you fine-tune parenting, it requires time. Unfortunately, when some parents become more efficient with their "child-time," they use the time saved for other *self*-fulfilling activities.

When my own children were young and I was working hard to build a child psychiatric practice, I was much less available to them than I am today. Sometimes when I am listening attentively, free of interruptions and distractions, to one of my child patients, I realize sadly what a unique experience this is for the child. Can you imagine the impact of both parents devoting one hour a week exclusively to listen to, understand, and enjoy each one of their children? Think what it would do for the child, and the parent-child relationship, if this were done weekly for the eighteen or nineteen years the child lived at home. Listening to children with care, and letting them know that their thoughts and feelings are of concern to you can be a vital step in maintaining a lifelong mutual relationship of respect and love.

The relationship of God the Father to the "children of Israel" described in the Old Testament provides helpful direction for parents. As the Old Testament describes the presence of God as being crucial to the growth and development of the people of Israel, so is the "presence" of the parents necessary to guide a child. How fortunate are children who have both *God* and *parents* at their side.

Children whose parents are available to them are more secure, confident, and happy. Having a parent at home provides more control over how a young child's life is structured. Children's personality and character should develop more steadily and smoothly when there is routine and consistency in their lives. Regular meals, nap time, bath time, prayer time, and bedtime are ways to provide structure for children. Putting routine into children's lives allows them to invest their energies in learning and relating to others, instead of trying to anticipate and adjust to a frantic and shifting environment.

Recently I evaluated Tommy, a five-year-old boy who had been expelled from two pre-schools because he was hyperactive, and had cursed and hit his teachers. He was also out-of-control at home, refusing to go to his bedroom to sleep, and running away when his parents corrected him. At mealtime Tommy would not eat anything but pizza and hotdogs and would disrupt the meal with demanding, belligerent behavior. The parents brought him for psychiatric evaluation, thinking he might have attention deficit disorder (ADD). Tommy was observed to be an energetic, athletic five-year-old with no obvious signs of an emotional problem. Ritalin was prescribed, largely to *rule out* the possibility his diagnosis was attention deficit disorder. As the medicine produced only slight improvement, I did not recommend that it be continued. Shortly after Tommy saw me, he left for Maine to stay with his maternal grandparents for one month. The following is a letter to Tommy's parents that they copied to me. The names of the parents (Nicole and Robert) and the grandparents (Alice and Frank) have been changed.

Nicole and Robert:

We would like to put into writing some of our thoughts after being involved with Tommy since the middle of May and most especially the past three weeks. Although we certainly are not experts in child behavior, nor do we claim to be perfect parents, the following will be our observations and suggestions regarding Tommy and what will work for him toward his future development.

The most significant thing we see is that he requires structure in his life. By that we mean he responds well to having scheduled mealtimes, bedtimes, specific types of playtime, quiet time upon approaching bedtime, etc. In doing this we have found that he will sleep in his own bed willingly. He goes to sleep peacefully after a bedtime story (with no television going). His excuses for not doing this in the beginning were numerous, and varied. We ignored them and proceeded with our program. At mealtime, he sits at the table with adults using his utensils and napkin, which is required, and eats what is put in front of him. This includes vegetables, fruit of all kinds, different meats, and soup. Milk is the mealtime drink. The only time he gets dessert is when he finishes his entire meal, and this is his decision.

We have tried and feel it works to reinforce consistent behavior. This means that we do, and he does, the same things the same way every time. Manners are part of this consistent behavior as well as treating other people the way you want to be treated in return. This also includes being very firm with him. If you say something is to be a certain way, you must carry through with it—because if you give him an inch, he'll take a mile every time. This also incorporates that he cannot be put in a position of negotiating, which he still attempts, but for the past three weeks, that program has absolutely not been allowed.

We have enjoyed having Tommy with us. For the most part, he's been a very happy and cooperative little guy—seemingly well adjusted to his three week visit with us without you or Robert. He's been very social, and has fit into every situation that we've exposed him to.

I hope this will help you—and I'm going to send a copy of this to Dr. Myers—hoping that all of this input will only help Tommy to fit into the big world that is waiting for him as he grows and matures.

Love,

Alice and Frank

Nicole and Robert said they had difficulty establishing family routine because their jobs were demanding and required long and inconsistent work hours. Both parents acknowledged they let most of Tommy's behavior go unchallenged because it was easier to let him have his way than to spend so much time arguing with him. When Tommy came in to see me after his visit with his grandparents, he was more relaxed and calmer than when I had seen him before. His parents said Tommy was now easier to control and he was sleeping in his own bed. All of us agreed Tommy did not have ADD and that Ritalin was not the answer for his problems. The focus of the therapy shifted to helping the parents establish more structure, routine, and consistency in their home.

Parents Must Sacrifice

Being a parent seldom requires the *magnitude* of sacrifice Jesus made for his children, but, done properly, it will require *considerable* sacrifice. Parents will find they can no longer be as pleasure-seeking as many of their single friends. Mothers who choose to have children should accept it *may limit* what might have been accomplished in a *career*. Likewise, a career *may limit* what can be accomplished as a *mother*. Both can easily require a *full-time* commitment. Being a mother *is* a career for millions of women, and there is what I consider a hopeful trend of mothers returning to the home.

Of course, many modern couples share parenting responsibility in ways that are far removed from the traditional "hunter" and "gatherer" stereotypes of our forefathers. In some families the female is the primary wage-earner, while the male remains at home to care for the children. Today there are varying blends of the traditional "mother" and "father" roles. The Bible does not specify that the emotional needs of children are to be met only by the mother. Jesus' comments and interactions with children seemed characteristic of the way a mother might relate. He was eager to have children around him and described children as models for learning how to approach God. He also related to his disciples, whom he called "children," with a "mothering" quality.

One of the advantages of the father taking on "mothering" responsibility is that it involves him more actively in the parenting process. It also makes him appreciate the labor and joys of motherhood. Such fathers are more supportive and helpful to their wives. Done wisely, blending parental responsibility gives both parents greater satisfaction and support. This provides a model for the children to emulate as they see their parents' helpfulness, respect, and love for one another.

Unfortunately, when some parents blend parental responsibility, *no one* chooses to be the "mother." Someone has to take this role.

True parental role reversals must be considered "experimental." The jury is still out on what type of adults will grow from such arrangements. There are thousands of years of experience with a "mother" being a woman. I tend to go along with that. Others might argue that the state of the world today suggests it is time for a change.

Well-intentioned couples may plan carefully how they can provide good care for a child without compromising either of their careers. If husband and wife decide they must skimp on their time with children, maybe they should reconsider whether they should have children at all. There are other opportunities, including Big

Brothers, volunteer work in child social agencies, coaching children's sports, and caring for a niece or nephew, by which an adult's maternal and paternal needs can be met. Popular slogans such as "I want it all," "I want to be my own person," "Just do it!" and "Go for it!" have a hollow ring when they are superimposed on shaping a child's life.

It certainly is possible to have a career *and* be a successful mother. However, skillful orchestration is necessary, and ideally there will be few unplanned crises such as illness, pregnancy, marital discord, or job transfers. There must be flexible working hours that will allow the mother to *first* respond to her children when there is a special and immediate need. It will increase chances of success if there is an understanding, supportive spouse who also has a job that lets him take time off to help. Remarkable judgment and good luck will be needed to choose child-care centers, baby-sitters, drivers, tutors, and other helpers who will be able to adequately replace a parent.

It would be interesting to compare the money made by both parents working during the first five years of a child's life, with the extra cost of caring for and treating an insecure and unhappy child. Maladjusted children require special services that can quickly eat away earlier savings. Consider the costs of psychological or educational testing, tutors, and special schools, in addition to child, family, and/or parental counseling. Should a child's difficulties progress to alcohol or drug abuse, depression, antisocial behavior, or other forms of mental illness, costs can become astronomical. Having a parent at home is a big advantage to a child. A decision for both parents to work in order to provide more material possessions for their children, or to provide their children with more stimulating life experiences, may be short-sighted and can be a mistake financially. There is little parents can provide their children that is more important than their *presence*. Money cannot replace it. The first five years are when the foundation, walls, and roof of children's personalities are being constructed; it is important that their carpenters (loving parents) are working on the job. "Subcontracting" child-rearing can lead to a shoddy result.

Be an Example

Jesus was an *example* for his disciples. Children identify with their parents. A child is like a recording camcorder or a sponge soaking up the personality of his or her parents. Proverbs 20:7 says, "It is a wonderful heritage to have an honest father." Whenever children are in the presence of their parents, they are making their parents' attitudes, values, beliefs, and approach to life part of themselves. Neither the parent nor the child fully appreciates that the child's camcorder is usually "on." Sometimes the "playback" of the parents' personalities does not demonstrate itself for years. Discovering we have developed mannerisms, thought patterns, and habits that belonged to our parents should be a clear signal, or warning, that our children are absorbing our own character. The child's camcorder will pick up important attitudes and beliefs of the parents, as well as minute, seemingly insignificant information. For example, I have seen several teenagers who have elaborately tattooed their bodies, justifying their action to their parents because one parent has a small, inconspicuous tattoo. Incidentally, it was a surprise to read in the Bible (Leviticus 19:28) that God forbids tattooing.

I am a morning jogger and regularly dodge parents who ignore stop signs as they drive their children to school. Those children also have their "camcorders" running. The parents may find that when these children begin driving, they disregard the parents' instructions to "stop for stop signs." Few parents stop to consider that by running a stop sign today they could endanger their teenage children ten years later.

Family interests may be passed down by identification. For example, a man is an avid golfer, and his grandfather and his father also played golf. Is it surprising that his son is on the high school golf team? None of these men ever told their sons to play golf. The sons just identified with their fathers.

My wife was raised in a family where many activities revolved around their church and the friends she made there. As an adult she continued to attend church regularly and was a good Christian role model for her children. Her children, my stepchildren, continue this religious heritage. Their children and their children's children will live their lives by Christian principles. What a wonderful gift to pass on to children!

Jesus was perfect as an *example* for his disciples. What he taught was entirely consistent with the way he thought, felt, and lived. As human parents we cannot be perfect, but we *can* appreciate that the example we set for our children will strongly influence them, and we *can try* to make our actions more consistent with what we "preach" to our children. Our children are likely to grow up emotionally healthy if we ourselves are better people and live our lives in a stable, consistent, obedient, and righteous manner. Being a good role model for your children will help them to become successful and satisfied adults more than any words you can ever say. I am convinced that the surest guide for being a good example is found through reading the Holy Bible. When parents model their lives from what can be learned in the Bible, it increases the odds of their being successful in that role. Living a life that is pleasing to God will automatically lead you to become a more effective parent. The behavior and values God demands and teaches for adults in the Bible are the same we want for our children. If *you* are obedient to the word of God, and are respectful, loving, kind, caring, industrious, and honest, your child will be more likely to develop these qualities.

Just as strongly, children will identify with *our bad example.* The most *certain* indicator I have found that children will abuse drugs is that their parents use them. Regardless of what they are taught, these children will view drug use as permissible. How can it be bad if the people they love, trust, and respect the most (their parents) do it? Even when parents use marijuana "recreationally," it can have disastrous consequences for their children. Parents who *seem* to have successful lives, yet use drugs, typically began their drug use *after* they were adults, already having accomplished many developmental tasks. For example, they have become comfortable with their sexual identity, dated, made friendships not based largely on mutual drug use, probably completed high school, and made progress in pursuing an education and/or gainful employment. However, their children will not be so fortunate. The children of these parents will begin using drugs *before* such tasks are accomplished. People who work with the mentally ill, with the homeless, and in child and adult courts can attest to the devastating disruption of a child's development if drug use begins during childhood and early adolescence.

Because marijuana is illegal, the parents who smoke it will generally associate with other people who have a compromised, personalized view of what is right and wrong. Such parents will avoid contact with people who would be critical of their drug use, therefore depriving the children of wholesome life experiences and positive influences that could help guide and direct them. For example, drug-using parents are less likely to take their children to church. Parents must never delude themselves into thinking they can hide their pot smoking from their children. Their "camcorders" see the truth.

Sometimes we have parts of our personality that are hidden, even to ourselves. Parents, without realizing it, can reinforce a child's behavior that consciously they are trying to extinguish. For example, a father may punish his son for spending so much of his time "chasing after girls," yet the father may secretly enjoy hearing of his son's sexual exploits. It is no wonder such a father is ineffective in controlling his son's behavior. The father's true thoughts and feelings influenced his son more than his words. "Do as I say and not as I do" has little place in child-rearing. Children identify with what we do and really are.

Protect, but Also Prepare

Jesus *protected* his disciples, but he also *prepared* them to *go out on their own*. The younger the child, the more intense is the level of protection and care that child must receive. An infant emerging from the womb comes into a world that, for the infant, is without form. The mother filters the overwhelming stimulation to the infant and "organizes" the chaos for him or her. She translates this "noise" of the environment into a logical pattern, and assists the infant to integrate these experiences with the feelings and sensations of his or her own body. Through this interaction, children first bond with their mother, learn the difference between what is real or fantasy, and develop a concept of well-being and basic trust. Later, the mother gradually allows the child to develop separateness from her and encourages the emergence of the child's independent identity. The mother's role, particularly during the child's infancy, is crucial. She protects and buffers her child from a harsh, sometimes dangerous, environment and prepares him or her for contact with the outside world. The loving interaction between a mother and her infant accomplishing the tasks described above is an excellent example of "quality time."

The younger the children are, the more *directly* parents can impact them. When children are young, parents have the best opportunity to modify children's behavior and character traits. As trees that grow crooked must be set straight while young, so children need attention early in life if they are to change. As early as one, two, or three years of age, parents can observe behaviors that signal future difficulties for their child. By three years of age, some children can be described as demanding, selfish, inflexible, angry, cruel, disrespectful, insatiable, unappreciative, dishonest, loners, unhappy, impulsive, risk-taking, stubborn, fearful, and countless other negative, as well as positive, attributes.

True, some of these characteristics represent a "stage" children are passing through. The problem with this assumption is some parents don't realize that children's successful passages through their "stage" are largely *determined* by *how* parents deal with the behavior. If a parent ignores and accepts a child's disrespectful behavior, the child may *never* pass through the stage of conflict with authority figures. Without caring, wise, determined parents to confront and shape children, they could stay in the "terrible twos" the rest of their lives.

Parents should see problem behaviors as an *opportunity* to correct unhealthy personality traits. Children have a natural tendency to want immediate pleasure and will resist when parents thwart their wishes; thus *conflict* will occur. Dealing with conflict is an important aspect of quality time. During early childhood, parents have power, influence, and control that will *not* exist in the future. The earlier parents confront and resolve difficulties with their children, the better.

Children have a natural tendency to gravitate toward dangerous activity and things that can cause character and moral defects. In Galatians 5:17–21, Paul says, "We naturally love to do evil things that are just the opposite from the things the Holy Spirit tells us to do." And he warns: "When you follow your own wrong inclinations, your lives will produce evil results such as impure thoughts, eagerness for lustful pleasure, idolatry, hatred and fighting, jealousy and anger, constant effort to get the best for yourself, complaints and criticism and the feeling that everyone is wrong except those in your own little group." "This," he says, "can lead to drunkenness, wild parties, and murder."

In *Lord of the Flies* by William Golding,[1] the children shipwrecked on an island without adult supervision soon revert to savages inflicting torment and murder upon one another. Child and adolescent gang behavior provides another example of unbridled child instincts. Gang members often have had no father with whom they could identify, or their father was ineffective in helping them control themselves. Children must be loved, protected, nurtured, and enjoyed. They must also be controlled, shaped, and taught to be civilized, law-abiding, God-fearing, compassionate human beings. The process that brings this about is *quality time.*

A family provides a base from which a child can safely test new skills. When there is inordinate risk for the child, parents must limit the child's exposure to danger. Although parents must protect their children, they must not interfere with them having experiences that develop competence and self-confidence. By cautiously allowing more independence and separation from the family, parents prepare children to go out on their own and make it possible for them to learn from others. Making the correct decision when to protect a child and when to let go is the *essence* of parenting. It is not an easy task and requires maturity, wisdom, and sometimes divine guidance.

Even if a parent understands the risks and advantages to a child, there are decisions that involve complex probabilities. Do you let your children walk to school by themselves? It will depend on the distance to the school, the traffic, the type of neighborhood, the weather, your child's intelligence, maturity, attention span, mood, the personalities of the children they will walk with, whether they are rushed to get to school that day, and numerous other factors. Many child-rearing decisions involve risk. What are the odds? Do you let your child play football? Go to camp? Get a hardship license? Spend the night with a friend? See an "R" rated movie? Car date? Drink alcohol at home? Smoke cigarettes? Try to control who their friends are? Set a strict curfew?

Repeated exposure to the same risk increases the probability of something bad happening. For example, if you let your children stay out until 2:00 AM on one night, there may be only one chance in fifty that they will get into trouble. If you let them stay out that late for fifty nights, there is a one hundred percent chance that they will get into trouble on one of those nights. This may be highly significant, because for teenagers today "getting into trouble" is not becoming involved in the harmless pranks of years past. Today "getting into trouble" can mean drug abuse, AIDS, or drive-by shooting.

Making and implementing crucial parenting decisions

requires parents to have spent enough time with their children to know their strengths and vulnerabilities. They must also know and assess their child's friends, since friends will strongly influence a child's behavior. It is helpful to have met their friends' parents so that a "united front" can be presented with the other parents if a particular activity or type of behavior of the children must be curtailed. Knowing the parents may also give you an indication of the value system of their children. Parents must know where their children are, what they are doing, and the degree of risk their activities entail. The process of obtaining this information and making the most correct decision for your child is also *quality time.* Parents' commitment only to "fun times" with their children is no substitute for the loving, but often unappreciated, effort parents put into making these decisions.

A seventeen-year-old girl begged her parents to let her spend the night with friends at a lake house where no adults would be present. When the parents refused, she argued that they weren't being "fair," inasmuch as she had never done anything that should cause them not to trust her. That was true. These parents had continually given their daughter freedom *only* to a degree that did not exceed her ability to handle it. They knew their daughter's strengths. They knew her friends. They permitted her few opportunities to disappoint them. However, if they had regularly let her stay overnight without adult supervision, it is almost certain that their daughter would have eventually given them a reason not to trust her. Parents must continually judge when to let their children go and when to secure them in their "base" of parental protection, direction, and control. Proverbs 22:6 says, "Teach a child to choose the right path, and when he is older he will remain on it."

The New Testament clarifies and expands upon the parenting directions stated in the Old Testament. Jesus also *taught* his children how to *save their souls.* For Christians, raising children to be competent, successful adults is not enough. It is when their children *also* accept the gift of immortal life offered through Jesus' sacrifice for them that Christian parents breathe a sigh of relief and *know,* "We have provided *quality time* for our children." Quality time with parents produces children who both love and respect their parents. God promises that when children honor their father and mother the children will have good and long lives.

CHAPTER SIX

Giving Your Child a Good and Long Life

The ten commandments (Exodus 20) give clear instruction on how we are to relate to God and to one another. Of these commandments, "Honor your father and mother" is unique. It is the only commandment that tells us "what *to* do" rather than "what *not* to do" in our human relationships. It is the only commandment giving directions specifically for family living. It is the only commandment that comes with a promise from God, for Exodus 20:12 says that if we honor our father and mother, we will "have a good and long life."

In Matthew 15:4 Jesus said, "Honor your father and mother; anyone who reviles his parents must die." Children who grow up failing to honor their parents violate a *direct commandment* of God. It has been my observation that such children will be undisciplined and have little respect for authority. They are often troubled, unhappy, and less likely to live the good and long life described in Exodus 20. Rebellious teenagers are particularly at risk. Homicide and suicide are leading causes of death among teenagers.

From my psychiatric perspective, next to "loving your child," "assuring that your child honors his or her father and mother" is the most crucial task parents can accomplish to protect their child from a troubled life. Children who are physically or sexually abused by parents suffer a handicap equally as damaging as the abuse itself, for these children will be unable to honor their parents. Honoring one's father and mother is the platform from which parents' discipline of their child should begin. Discipline of children is weakened or ineffective if children have no respect for their parents.

Failure of children to honor their father or mother can begin as early as the first year of life. During the first year, children should pass through their stage of absolute dependency and become more separate from their parents. In a natural and gradual fashion, parents teach their children that they are not in command of the world. However, some parents, intent on meeting the needs of their children, do not permit their children to be separate. These parents continue to function as if they are an extension of their infant. Every cry is quickly soothed by over-eager parents. An infant may conclude that parents live exclusively to meet his or her needs. As children get older, they will not honor their father and mother if they continue to control their parents. Fortunately, life circumstances usually interfere with the development of such a pathological parent-child relationship. Parents have other demands on their time that keep them from perpetually over-gratifying their infant. However, mild "child control" over a parent is common.

Who Is in Charge?

Parents who are not aware of biblical direction may have no clear standard for setting a child's values and character. Their interactions with their children are largely driven by what makes the children happy. This can give children unhealthy power over their parents.

A child's sense of power may be perpetuated by parents unknowingly. For example, today's parents spend a significant amount of time with their children in a car. While transporting children, parents may be so preoccupied with their own thoughts that they neglect to have their children honor and obey them. This is dangerous in a moving car, as well as psychologically unhealthy.

Allowing children to ignore their parents while the parents drive them to activities can undermine parental authority. It is common for children to arrive at my office asleep in the back seat of the car. Other times the children arrive listening to music with head phones, ensuring that they did not have to talk to "their driver." Routinely permitting such behavior confirms to a child that "what a parent has to say" is unimportant. Car time can be an excellent opportunity for parents and child to talk to each other. Insisting that a child pay attention and engage the parent in conversation creates more respect for the parent and also shows the child that the parent values his or her ideas and opinions.

Sometimes parents are so self-sacrificing that it causes the children to have an unrealistic approach to life. Parents who themselves endured hardship and/or neglect as children may be too intent on seeing that their child does not "go through what they went through." Parents who spend little time with their children may try to make it up to them by over-indulging them. The parent will regularly give the child special consideration and then wait nervously to see if the child is pleased. I recently observed a young couple's doting interaction with their three-year-old daughter in an expensive restaurant. They would carefully select the choicest morsel on their plates and would wait anxiously to see if she would accept their "gift." The parents would open their mouths with each bite they presented their child and wait in fearful anticipation to see if the child would reject the morsel. Even a casual observer would identify this child as being in the "honored" position. It is understandable how such a child could come to feel her rights are superior to her parents.

Children who are over-indulged can feel so special and privileged that they become condescending and inconsiderate with other children and adults. Even if parents are comfortable jumping to satisfy the demands of their own children, other adults will be critical of the children's attitude and behavior. These children irritate and anger others, and they will find the outside world unfriendly and rejecting. The child's response to this rejection can vary, from changing his or her attitude and becoming sensitive to authority, to living a life of alienation and conflict. However, few children act like tyrants at home and become respectful to adults when they are away. Most children do not have the discernment, or self-control, to act one way with family and another way when away from home.

Parents need not provide the "best" for the child instead of themselves. What incentive do children have to work to achieve the things their parents have when they grow up being *given* many privileges of adulthood? It is not selfish for the parent to take the "choice" portion, own a better bicycle or automobile than their child, or go to Europe when their child hasn't been there. It is understandable why some children grow up feeling that they, not their parents, should be honored.

Some parents feel embarrassed and guilty if they give preferred treatment to themselves over their children. Even very young children will exploit their parents' guilt to gain power and control. At a later age the children will remain convinced they should smoke, drink alcohol, own a car, and stay out late simply because "their parents do it." They don't consider age, experience, education, or having earned a right as relevant because they were reared from infancy with the idea they were equal to their parents. I know a seventeen-year-old boy who has been driving his own car since age fifteen, but will only go to the family vacation home if he is allowed to fly while his parents drive and pick him up at a nearby airport. He does not like to drive there because "it is boring." He will not help to pack or unload the car. He says the parents are using *"his* time," school vacation, to do something the parents want to do for themselves, not him. Allowing such entitled behavior causes the son to have little respect for his parents.

Establishing Authority

What can a parent do to gain honor and respect? The first step in developing a biblically-directed relationship with your child is to accept "honor your father and mother" as a goal for your child without apology. It is a natural, healthy, and godly phenomenon.

Being "honored" carries a responsibility some parents want to avoid. It may be a signal to these parents that they are really "grown up." It does not allow them to be the child's playmate and it emphasizes their parental role. Having a child may *force* a parent to mature. 1 Corinthians 13:11 says, "When I was a child I thought and spoke and reasoned as a child does. But when I became a man my thoughts grew far beyond those of my childhood, and now I have put away the childish things." Parents may need to change some of their own attitudes and behaviors. For example, it may be more difficult to teach your child respect for authority if you yourself are weak in this area. Parents can help each other with this. If a child is disrespectful to his or her mother, the father should quickly intervene, and vice versa. Parents, by the way they relate to each other, should demonstrate an attitude of honor and respect. If parents speak rudely to each other, the child may do the same.

Parents will not need to look to find ways they can

demonstrate their authority to their child. A child's natural egocentric attitude will clash with the needs of other family members, and conflict is inevitable. To children's dismay, they realize *parents* decide when children wake up, when and what they eat, when they bathe, and what time they go to bed. Parents who can implement such routines ensure that their child gets adequate sleep, exercise, and nutrition, and has good personal hygiene. Settling these issues early in a child's life will greatly decrease whining, crying, temper tantrums, colds, finicky eating, fatigue, tardiness, arguments, procrastination, and other forms of behavior that can be annoying and tiring to parents. Setting a child's routine is no small accomplishment. I *commonly* see parents of teenagers who are *still* struggling with where and when their teenager will *sleep, eat* and *bathe.*

Recently I saw a six-year-old girl who had been referred because of behavior problems at school. In the process of getting routine information about the family, I learned the girl always slept in the den on the sofa, rather than in her bedroom. Her mother explained that the daughter liked to go to sleep watching TV in the den and cried if the mother tried to make her sleep in her own bed. The parents decided it was less trouble to let their daughter stay in the den than trying to convince her to go to her room. The mother was perplexed when I said this behavior should be confronted, and she asked, "What difference does it make where you sleep, *if* you sleep?" Later that day, I saw a patient whose behavior answered that question. A seventeen-year-old boy had slipped out of his house and spent the night at his girlfriend's, unbeknownst to her parents. When I asked him why he did this, his response was, "What difference does it make where you sleep, as long as you sleep?"

In the process of establishing simple routines of sleep, nutrition, exercise, and hygiene for a pre-schooler, parents set the ground rules for how he or she will accept authority for the rest of his or her life. Parents who do not accomplish these tasks during the child's early years subject themselves and their children to a difficult and uncertain future.

Teaching children manners helps them to show respect for others. Having children say "yes sir," "thank you," "please," and "excuse me," take off their hats in the house, keep their feet off the furniture, and practice other social courtesies can be an indicator of how well they are learning their parents' values. Some parents feel that manners are old-fashioned and outdated. However, manners will never hurt a child. The same cannot be said for rude and disrespectful behavior.

I regularly see the sad result of parents ignoring, postponing, or hoping *someone else* will teach their child to respect authority. Proverbs 19:26 says, "A son who mistreats his father or mother is a public disgrace." Children who do not respect their parents may become a discredit to themselves *and* their parents.

Parents should not permit a child to be verbally disrespectful to them or to *any adult.* Calling parents or grandparents degrading names, even in a playful fashion, is not helpful, as children will have difficulty understanding this is less acceptable when they get older.

Children should never hit their parents. Even infants can understand that hitting parents is not acceptable.

Defiance

Putting off confronting a child's defiance will make the job increasingly more difficult. It is much easier to teach a child you are more powerful *if you are.* Contrast how you might manage a three-year-old child who spits in your face, compared to a *seventeen*-year-old child who spits in your face. Parents too easily ignore or deny their child's disobedient and disrespectful behavior. Too many parents of the "Now Generation" want cable television, a VCR, car telephone, stylish clothes, and travel, and they want it *now.* These same parents *also* expect their children to obey, honor, and respect them *now.* If their child's honor and respect does not come *quickly* and *easily,* some parents abandon the effort to train their child.

It may take years and hundreds of struggles with a particularly strong-willed child before the parents can establish their authority. These conflicts are an opportunity to teach your child to respect authority while you still have the power and control. When reprimanding your children, insist that they *look you in the eyes, listen to you,* and *acknowledge* they *understand* and *accept* your authority. No matter how unpleasant, time-consuming, and difficult this teaching seems when he or she is young, it will *never* get easier.

It is natural for young children to question their parents' authority. However, there is a difference between listening to a child in order to understand and teach him or her, and allowing a child to ignore and/or defy a parent. As a child's personality develops there will be times when the conflict between what the child wants and parental limits will escalate into the child becoming defiant. Both from a psychiatric and a biblical perspective, confronting child defiance is an essential feature of learning to respect authority.

Parents will never have their children's respect if they let the children defy them. Child-rearing allows many opportunities for power struggles, arguing, and a child exerting his or her independence. Blatant defiance by a child should *not* be tolerated.

"Defiance" means a child's behavior is out control, that a parent cannot reason with the child, and the child refuses to obey. Such situations generally occur in early childhood. Physical intervention may become necessary for the parent to protect the child or others, and to re-establish parental control. Often this can be done by holding or restraining the child. Sometimes spanking may be necessary.

Spanking

Recently in an adolescent psychotherapy group, I jokingly made the remark, "Santa might bring switches," to one of the group members. My comment was met by blank stares. None of the seven members knew a definition for the word other than the type of "switch" used to turn on an electric light or a computer. Few of my child and adolescent patients report they were ever spanked.

The Bible says that spanking is an acceptable method for dealing with a child's defiance.

Proverbs 13:24: "He who spares the rod hates his son, but he who loves him is careful to discipline him."

Proverbs 22:15: "Folly is bound up in the heart of a child, but the rod of discipline will drive it far from him."

There are some parents who are so immature, so troubled, and so unstable that they have neither the discernment nor the self-control to safely use spanking as a method for teaching and protecting their children. However, these parents are not the majority. Unfortunately, normal parents who may occasionally spank a child are too often painted by the same brush that depicts mentally unstable, sociopathic parents.

Normal, loving parents do not spank a child to relieve their own frustrations. Such parents will take into account extenuating circumstances that may have led to a child's defiant behavior. These parents use physical means of discipline only when other methods are not effective, when the child remains defiant, and when permitting the child's behavior to continue would be harmful to the child or others.

Being physical with a young child on such rare occasions is a loving and protecting act. It is not "abuse." It is painful for parents to have to resort to such measures. The old adage, "This is hurting me more than it is hurting you," reflects the proper state of mind for parents who must spank their child.

For some young children who do not understand consequences, a spanking may be necessary. It is certainly better for a child to learn that running into the street will cause a "spanking" than that "streets are dangerous" from being hit by a car. From my experience as a psychiatrist and as a father, there is a place for spanking in child-rearing. Scripture says it is permissible, and at times indicated. Proverbs 23:13–14: "Don't fail to correct your children; discipline won't hurt them! They won't die if you use a switch on them! Punishment will keep them out of hell."

The older the child, the less likelihood spanking will be useful. It is particularly questionable to spank a child who has entered puberty. Although parents may perceive their young adolescents as children, adolescents have many adult feelings and can consider a spanking an assault. Getting physical with an emotionally disturbed adolescent can be dangerous. One fifteen-year-old adolescent killed both his parents after being wrestled to the ground by his father. If your children require spanking, it should be administered in their early years.

It is *crucial* that a child learn to honor his or her father and mother by the time the child is five years of age. Many parents can accomplish this without spanking. However, if it is necessary, it is certainly better to spank a child than to permit your child to grow up without respect for authority.

The Bible gives parents authority over their children and says parents are accountable to God should they misuse this trust. Jesus said in Matthew 18:6, "But if any of you causes these little ones who trust in me to lose their faith, it would be better for you to have a rock tied to your neck and be thrown into the sea." Governmental laws also hold parents responsible if they neglect or abuse a child. The parents' job is to teach their children to respect authority. God and the courts will take action should the parents abuse this power.

Being Best Friends

Parents sometimes feel they must relate to their children in the same manner that they do to each other. The parents worry that being authoritative will cause their children to feel inferior and have low self-esteem. This is not a self-esteem issue. Parents who treat their children like children are relating appropriately. It is a disservice to their children to do otherwise, inasmuch as it denies the reality that there is a difference. Parents and children are *not* equal. Nowhere in the Bible are parents advised to be a "friend" of their child. It erodes respect for parents to relate predominantly as a friend to their child, since a child does not recognize the authority of his or her friend. Being your child's best friend may also delay the child taking the risk of making friends of his or her own age. It may prolong dependence on parents and make it more difficult for the child to develop a separate identity.

When a parent (usually the mother) considers her child (usually the daughter) her "best friend," it often also indicates there is an alliance exclusive of the other parent (usually the father). This is destructive to the parents' relationship with each other and causes the child to have less respect for their authority. Adolescents who are *too* close to a parent may eventually have to use extraordinary effort to become independent. Acting out behaviors such as outlandish physical appearance and dress, defiance, drug and alcohol use, and sexual promiscuity may be the only way the teenager knows to break away from a smothering parent. The degree of teenage rebellion sometimes seems linked to the degree of apparent "closeness" between parent and child.

Not long ago I met with a fourteen-year-old boy who was referred to me because of a learning problem and signs of an attention deficit disorder. He was a polite, friendly adolescent who was mildly depressed because he was making bad grades. At the end of our appointment, his parents came into the office with us. The boy got to his feet and gave the preferred seat on the sofa to his parents. In *thirty years* of the practice of child psychiatry, it was the first time I had ever seen this happen! By this simple act, the boy demonstrated his respect for his parents. I am sure there must be many families where such an occurrence is common. Perhaps these families less often end up in a psychiatrist's office.

If your children enter kindergarten having firmly established an attitude of respect for their parents, they will *continue* to demonstrate respect for other authority figures. They will be appreciated by other parents, teachers, and peers. They will be ready to devote their energies to learning, rather than struggling with teachers over authority issues that should have been *already* settled by parents. Children who honor their father and mother should adjust well to school, since they have been *prepared* to accept discipline.

CHAPTER SEVEN

Discipline as Love

Discipline goes hand-in-hand with teaching children to honor their father and mother. Parents who are honored by their children spend less time and effort disciplining them. Similarly, parents who use discipline wisely will be honored by their children. The book of Proverbs, written primarily by King Solomon, has been described as a guide for being successful in life. It contains many recommendations on how to parent a child. Solomon tells us that the way a child is raised will define his or her personality and character as an adult, and he stressed the importance of disciplining children:

Proverbs 3:11–12: "Young man, do not resent it when God chastens and corrects you, for his punishment is proof of his love. Just as a father punishes a son he loves to make him better, so the Lord corrects you."

Proverbs 19:18: "Discipline your son in his early years while there is hope. If you don't, you will ruin his life."

From the New Testament, consider Hebrews 12:7: "Let God train you, for he is doing what any loving father does for his children. Whoever heard of a son who was never corrected?" and Hebrews 12:11: "Being punished isn't enjoyable while it is happening—it hurts! But afterward we can see the result, a quiet growth in grace and character."

Permissive Parenting

Child psychiatrists have an undeserved reputation of encouraging permissive parenting. We, of all people, realize the great harm done to children when their parents do not discipline. Such children frequently become our patients with symptoms of temper tantrums, defiance, rage, low frustration tolerance, depression, vandalism, criminality, poor school adjustment, and drug use. According to the Bible *and* psychological theory, discipline is an essential feature of parent/child interaction. It should be administered as a part of parents' *love* for their child. God told John in Revelation 3:19, "I continually discipline and punish everyone I love." Solomon in Proverbs 13:24 says, "If you refuse to discipline your son, it proves you don't love him; for if you love him you will be prompt to punish him."

It has been my experience that adults who seem the most consistently loving to others and who have the best relationship with their own parents were raised in homes where discipline was clear, fair, and firm. These adults do not look back on their childhood as harsh or abusive. They tell with amusement and fondness of times when they as children were disciplined by parents for bad behavior. There is a sense of pride in their parents and themselves for the lessons they learned. Proverbs 29:17 says, "Discipline your son and he will give you happiness and peace of mind." On the other hand, I have seen young children and adolescents who have not been disciplined and they *despise* their parents. In 1 Kings 1:6, the explanation for King David's son, Adonijah, turning against his father was that "King David had never disciplined him at any time."

Conscience and Consequences

Psychiatrists believe children may develop consciences from the way they are disciplined by their parents. When children mature, their parents remain in their unconscious minds ready to admonish them with guilt if they begin to do something wrong. It is ironic that some parents avoid punishing their children, feeling the children will identify with the parents' harshness and will grow up to be overly aggressive or violent adults. To the contrary, these parents may raise children who have little or no conscience, commonly seen in cruel and unlawful adults. Proverbs 29:15 says, "Scolding and spanking a child helps him to learn. Left to himself, he'd bring shame to his mother." Proverbs 29:19 adds: "Sometimes mere words are not enough—discipline is needed, for the words may not be heeded."

Discipline, administered with love, is a tool parents

should use to "civilize" their children, preparing them for safe, successful lives after they leave home. Just as a cute little puppy without training will grow into an unruly and unwelcome adult animal, so may an adorable young child, without proper discipline, live an adult life of alienation and rejection. Discipline enables us to teach our children, in our safe and loving homes, that there are *consequences* for their actions.

Emotionally healthy children begin to experience discipline early in life. When an infant becomes excessively demanding and aggressive, like throwing a bottle down on the floor or having a tantrum, the mother shows her displeasure. She supports or rewards her child's behavior depending on her judgment of its appropriateness. This requires the mother to be comfortable with allowing some frustration of the infant. Her action clearly translates to the child that she is in control of their relationship. This is the way discipline begins. Parents who themselves are insecure and fear criticism from a spouse or others may have difficulty setting limits for their child. Also, parents who spend little time with their child may be reluctant to discipline, wanting their child to "be happy" during the relatively brief time parent and child are together.

If children honor and respect their parents, discipline is relatively easy. Children want to please their parents and are uncomfortable if their parents show disapproval. Punishment can be a facial expression, a gesture, or words. As children get older, these expressions of parental disapproval are often reinforced when the parents deprive their children of something enjoyable.

Common examples are grounding, being restricted to their room, and no television. Punishments used by parents sometimes are ineffective, as they tend to be poorly thought out, unimaginative, and repetitive.

Discipline Suggestions

- When practical, let children learn from the natural consequences of their behavior. For example, rather than arguing with children that they will need a coat to be warm, let the cold teach them this lesson.

- Parents should avoid depriving children of an activity that is constructive. If children have trouble making friends, it is self-defeating to punish them by not letting them go to another child's birthday party or to baseball practice. If possible, a parent should take away activities that the parent does not particularly approve of. Examples might be depriving them of watching television, or eating candy and ice cream.

- It is more meaningful if the punishment can be related to the offense. If children abuse phone time, it is logical to ground them from the phone or remove the phone from their room. I know one parent who disciplines her children for not writing thank-you notes by taking away their present until the note is written. Other parents make their child give a toy to charity when their child is intentionally destructive. Taking toys away from children and returning them only after they keep their room picked up for a certain number of days is an example of this strategy.

- Try having your children "*do*" rather than "not do" something as a punishment. Grounding or depriving children of something they like is the most frequent punishment parents use. The penal system, notorious for being *in*effective for correcting bad behavior, relies on a similar system. Teachers and coaches, however, often use action-based punishment to help children learn from their errors. Examples are having children run laps, do push-ups, or copy a sentence repeatedly. Parents can use similar techniques. Examples I have seen include having the child clean the garage, wash windows, weed flower beds, paint, clean closets, polish shoes, and wash the car. One parent had his son write a theme on the dangers of sneaking out at night.

- Work that is used as punishment should be constructive. Children can write spelling words, do math problems, memorize Bible verses, or do other intellectual work they tend to avoid. These "punishments" give the child a sense of accomplishment. The "punishments" should be *in addition to,* and not replace, routine chores.

- "Do something" discipline may be avoided by parents because it requires time and effort. It is much easier, *in the short term,* to send a child to his or her room or take away TV privileges than to monitor a constructive activity. Parents who use "do something" discipline will need to enforce, instruct, direct, and supervise their child's effort. The parent/child interaction involved in this process can be true *quality time* for your child.

- Punishment should be used sparingly and wisely. Ephesians 6:4 says, "Don't keep on scolding and nagging your children, making them angry and resentful." Children may *become* defiant if the parents' discipline is blatantly unreasonable or too harsh. Parents who set punishments that are overly severe tend *not* to enforce them. The end result is a child who is *less* regularly disciplined.

- Except in cases where a child is in serious danger of hurting himself or another person, parents should avoid administering punishment in public or in front of a child's friends. This may humiliate children so severely that they will defy their parents.

- After an upsetting conflict, it is usually best to delay giving punishment until you and/or the child have calmed down. Punishing children when they are *already* severely distraught can cause defiance. On the other hand, if parent and child are in control, it is preferable to discipline a child soon after the act. Some children forget why they are being punished if discipline is too delayed.

- No discipline should be used that children will not obey or which the parents cannot enforce. Parents must make a judgment where this point occurs. I may advise parents to hold back from punishing a child when it is clear the parents do not have, or do not want to use, the power to enforce their discipline. For example, it is ludicrous to use grounding as a punishment when a teenager regularly defies the parents by leaving home without permission.

- Parents who have not spent much time with their children may not have enough information to make sound judgments about discipline. This can cause discipline to be confused, inconsistent, and unwisely administered. Small matters can escalate into severe crises that can have devastating effects on a family. Parents should be consistent in the way they discipline. Good communication between parents promotes consistent discipline and decreases the possibility of the child avoiding punishment by playing one parent against the other.

- Punishment should not require children to enforce the consequences of their behavior upon themselves. For example, parents sometimes ground children from watching TV and then let them spend the night with a friend. Most children do not have the maturity to inform friends they are restricted from TV. Disobeying their parents, children will go ahead and watch TV and then lie about what they did at their friend's house. It would have been better for the parents to limit children's TV time at home only.

Discipline is only one way a child's personality is shaped. The impact of parents being positive role models for their children has been emphasized in Chapter

Five. Loving, encouraging reward of a child's positive behavior is equally important. Although children understand there are consequences if they are bad, they seldom appreciate that their privileges will increase when they are *good*. It would be helpful if parents verbalized this connection. Examples might include: "You have been so helpful and obedient this week, why don't you invite a friend to go to the movie with us tonight?" or "You have been keeping your room so neat, I would like to get a new bedspread for you." or "You have been so polite recently, I would like to do something special with you." There are repeated examples in the Bible where individuals, cities, and nations are rewarded for their devotion to God and good works. Children can benefit from a similar program.

The Bible does not instruct us how to "reward" or "punish" children in specific situations. There are numerous secular books on child-raising that discuss specific methods and techniques: James Dobson's book, *The New Dare to Discipline,*[1] provides a particularly useful Christian perspective.

God holds parents responsible for providing discipline for their children. In 1 Samuel 2, Eli, a high priest and judge of Israel, did not discipline his children. God punished Eli by causing his children to "live in sadness and grief." *Humans* also judge us by how we manage our family. Paul wrote in 1 Timothy 3:4 that a pastor must "have a well-behaved family with children who obey quickly and quietly. For if a man can't make his own little family behave, how can he help the whole church?" Like it or not, how parents control their children is considered a reflection of how well they manage other aspects of their lives. Loving discipline is a missing ingredient in many homes today. Putting discipline back into child-rearing is psychologically healthy and biblically sound and should reap benefits for children *and* their parents. There is no substitute for parents' loving discipline.

CHAPTER EIGHT

Education Is Not *the* Answer

In 2 Chronicles 1:11–12, God said to Solomon, "Because your greatest desire is to help your people, and you haven't asked for personal wealth and honor, and you haven't asked me to curse your enemies, and you haven't asked for a long life, but for wisdom and knowledge to properly guide my people—yes, I am giving you the knowledge and wisdom you asked for! And I am also giving you such riches, wealth, and honor as no other king has ever had before you! And there will never again be so great a king in all the world!"

Can you imagine the satisfaction and sense of well-being his parents, King David and Bathsheba, must have felt watching Solomon grow into a man? If ever a man would be able to make the right choices it would be their son Solomon, the most knowledgeable man in the world.

Unfortunately, even a wise man may choose to be disobedient. Even though Solomon well understood the consequences of ungodly behavior, he drank excessively, womanized, and became egotistical and cynical. Solomon, the wisest man on earth, spent much of his later life disillusioned and in despair. In Ecclesiastes 2:20–23, Solomon reflects upon his life, "So I turned from hard work as the answer to my search for satisfaction. For though I spend my life searching for wisdom, knowledge, and skill, I must leave it all to someone who hasn't done a day's work in his life; he inherits all my efforts, free of charge. This is not only foolish but unfair. So what does a man get for all his hard work? Days full of sorrow and grief, and restless bitter nights. It is all utterly ridiculous."

If knowledge could not protect a "Solomon" from making self-destructive choices, we should not count on knowledge being adequate protection for our children. Moses in Deuteronomy 4:9–10 tells parents to teach their children to "know God's miracles, to fear God, and to learn his laws." The Bible does not say to educate children and then let them make their own decisions.

"Teaching your child to make the right choices" has become a guiding principle for today's parents. In my opinion, *over-reliance* on children being taught to "make the right choices" is often misguided and sometimes dangerous. Parents can expose their children to increased risk when they assume that what children *learn* will protect them. This can happen when parents and educators teach children, "Just say no," to sex, alcohol, drugs, and riding with strangers, *instead* of adequately supervising them. Although it is reasonable to work toward educating children to make safe decisions, it is foolhardy to think youngsters will regularly have enough discernment to protect themselves.

Children can learn a concept *before* they have the maturity or self-control to use it. For example, four-year-olds may understand that if they go out of their yard, they may be harmed. Despite this knowledge, they may impulsively dart into the street. Some concepts require a certain maturity before a child can actually put what is learned into practice. Most children do not understand that death is truly permanent until they are about eight years old. Parents certainly cannot rely on children knowing they can be killed as a deterrent, if the children do not appreciate that death is final.

Factors Other Than Education

- Often children's "right choice" is influenced more by their respect and fear of punishment from parents than by knowledge about the dangerous consequences of behavior. I asked a teenage boy, after he had seen a film of an accident caused by speeding in which both the driver and his girlfriend were killed, if he would speed. He responded, "No way, man! If I got a speeding ticket, my parents would take the car away."

- Children may follow the example of their parents, regardless of what others teach them. Lectures to a son on being respectful to women may be ineffective if he has a chauvinistic father. Parents are powerful role models for their children. Jesus in the tenth chapter of the gospel of John described how his "sheep" recognized his voice and followed him rather than strangers. Do you, as a parent, present values that are recognized and followed by your children? There is no academic lesson superior to a parent's life example in shaping a child's future.

- Children with few moral values make different decisions than those who have strong consciences. A conscience is a very useful part of a child's personality. It causes a child to automatically resist "bad" behavior in order to avoid a feeling of guilt. The parents "in their head," their conscience, help children make constructive decisions. There is nothing psychologically or biblically wrong with children doing "what is right" simply because it makes them feel better.

- Research in brain chemistry has shown drugs and/or alcohol trigger pleasure and reward signals that can overpower the judgment and "common sense" functions of the cerebral cortex. (Many of us could have told them this without the expense of research.) No matter how smart children are, their choices, like adults' choices, are *different* when they are under the influence of drugs and alcohol.

- The "right choice" for a child is also determined by the attractiveness of the temptation and by the setting. A boy will understand the risks of sneaking out, consistently turn down invitations to do it, and then go if a special person asks him. A girl may have been taught the consequences of having sex, resolve to remain a virgin until marriage, and yet give in if she is spending the night at a hotel party and has been drinking. Some situations have more appeal to certain individuals than to others. A teenager with a high genetic predisposition for alcoholism may have more difficulty choosing not to excessively drink alcohol.

- Children are highly influenced by peer pressure. Smoking is a good example. Children usually are well informed about the dangers of smoking. If parents smoke, their child may beg them to give up cigarettes. The same child, however, may quickly succumb to peer pressure when offered a cigarette by a friend. The futility of relying heavily on education to assure a child's "right choices" is probably *best* demonstrated by using smoking as an example. Why do millions of adults who are fully educated about the hazards of smoking continue to smoke? If education about the risks of a particular act does not stop *adults,* then why should we rely on education to *control children's* behavior? The problem is not that children don't know better; it is that they either cannot or do not want to stop.

- Children's emotional state will influence their choices. Children with attention deficit disorder (ADD) are impulsive and often act before thinking, even if they have fully learned and understood the consequences. Teenagers, and even young children, may suffer from depression. A child's mood will affect the ability to use information he or she has learned.

- Teenagers' appreciation of risk will be weakened by a belief they are beyond harm, a common adolescent idea. Despite understanding the consequences of speeding, not paying attention, and drinking, or even after losing friends in automobile accidents, teenagers may continue to drink and drive recklessly. They understand the risk, but they don't see it as applicable to themselves.

The Responsibility to Protect

Few children can cope with today's complicated, sinful, and dangerous life circumstances without the control and guidance of attentive parents. I have seen parents who act as if their responsibility to protect young children ends when they get them to understand not to pet a strange dog, swim without their parents, or go into the street. Do they really believe children can *consistently* follow these instructions? Children must have the ongoing protection of their parents, regardless of how well children understand concepts. Studies on the sexual abuse of children demonstrate that few children are able to resist the seductive power of an experienced child molester. A parent should not be less vigilant when their eight-year-old understands, "It is not good to let someone touch you in your private parts." Does knowing this mean a child should be allowed to go to movies, malls, or video game parlors unattended by parents?

It is discouraging to watch program planners repeatedly turn to *more* education for children to stop drug and alcohol abuse, end teenage pregnancy, avoid sexual abuse, get them to practice safe sex, and drive safely. Having children make an "A" in a course on these topics should not lessen a parent's responsibility to protect them. Children get into trouble and parents blame, and even sometimes sue, schools for not educating their children well enough to keep them safe. There is some pressure even to have schools teach morality. Teaching moral values in school might not be a bad idea if it was done *in addition to,* rather than *instead of,* the parents teaching their children right from wrong. The same can be said about school prayer. If parents prayed regularly with their children at home, whether or not they were exposed to it at school would be relatively inconsequential. School prayer becomes a crucial issue when the *only* experience a child has with God is what he or she hears on the school public address system. Unfortunately, some parents depend on schools not only to educate their children, but also to protect, control, and give them a value system.

Why do we so readily and naively accept education of children as a substitute for parenting? Are parents lazy? It is certainly easier in the short run to teach children the consequences and then let them look out for themselves. Are parents selfish? Are parents so interested in themselves that they jump at the opportunity to pass responsibility for their children to others, even the children themselves? Are parents today so stressed they have little energy available for child-raising? Are parents responding to peer pressure and letting their children have so much unsupervised freedom because "other parents are doing it"? Some parents justify providing less care because they are "helping their child learn to be independent." This can be a dangerous rationalization.

When to Let Go

Successful parents *protect* their children to whatever degree is necessary *until* the children demonstrate an ability to *regularly* make choices that are safe. This requires parents to make thousands of judgments that will affect the course of their children's lives. The parents must take into consideration the maturity of the child as well as the likelihood and the severity of the risk. To do this, they must truly know and understand the level of their children's intelligence, judgment, self-control, mood, and the way they are influenced by others. This means the parent must know their child's friends and have some idea about the friends' values and behavior. The parents must have information on planned activities and appreciate what risk each presents. The parent can then decide what level of responsibility will be given to the children and how much protection will be necessary. The choices *parents* make, not what choices the child makes, will largely determine how safely and successfully the child reaches adulthood.

Children should continually be given the opportunity to master new tasks and to handle responsibility. Each time children face and overcome a difficult or dangerous situation, they become wiser, stronger, and more competent. However, parents must dish out these opportunities in "bites" their children can safely and successfully "chew."

The parents' ability to correctly make these "calls" for their children is a hallmark of good parenting.

The process is analogous to coaching a rookie quarterback in the NFL. You can't just *teach* him the plays and send him onto the field. In addition to the teaching, he must *practice* under the scrutiny and support of his coach. He will be allowed *limited* playing time, under relatively *controlled* circumstances, with the coach calling the plays. Only when he has demonstrated *repeated* evidence that he is competent is the rookie given control. Putting him onto the field before he is adequately prepared would endanger him.

The same is true for children. Like the NFL quarterback, a child will eventually reach a level of maturity that will allow more responsibility for making his or her "own choices." However, this should be when children can demonstrate they are competent to *routinely* make safe decisions in the life circumstances they face. Parental responsibility should not be transferred to the child merely when the child, or teenager, or even young adult, has simply been "educated" about the risks and consequences. It should be transferred when children will safely *use* the information, not just *know* it.

Safely raising children to become God fearing, loving, moral, emotionally stable, competent adults is no easy task; however, it is possible. Millions of parents continue to do it; some just give up too easily. A parent must draw strength, support, and guidance from many sources to make wise judgments for their children. Reading the Bible offers insights of great value. The description of God in the Old Testament and Christ in the New Testament as shepherds seems a useful analogy for raising children. David, in Psalm 23, referred to the Lord as "a shepherd who provides for me, leads me to be righteous, and protects me from danger." When parents rely too heavily on protecting their children by teaching them to make the right choices, they actually put their children at risk. How long will sheep survive without the protection of a shepherd? What will happen to your children if you do not shepherd them?

Being a "shepherd" for your children is not a glamorous job. Good shepherds have few distractions, so they focus on caring for their flock. I have never heard of wealthy shepherds. If shepherds were wealthy, wouldn't they hire someone else to care for the sheep so they could go into town? Wealth could lessen their motivation for shepherding. Wealth could be perilous for their sheep.

CHAPTER NINE

The Perils of Wealth

Surprisingly, some families' most *un*happy times come during a family vacation. A typical scenario involves afflu-ent parents who have previously provided expensive, elab-orate, mini-vacations for their family. On this particular summer the parents decide to spend the family vacation in a modest cabin in the mountains or on the beach. The children complain from the beginning about the trip. They say the parents are mean because they have not arranged for the children to bring a friend with them. They don't like having to wait at the airport and complain that the drive in the rental car is too long. They resent having to wait while the parents buy groceries. They say the cabin is too hot and they refuse to share a room with their brother. The remainder of the week they whine, grumble, and try to make their parents miserable for bringing them on such a "boring" trip. However, it is not their children's attitudes or behavior that discourage the parents, as they have grown accustomed to their children's rudeness; it is, rather, the way the family members are treating each other in Cabin 2. Each family member in Cabin 2 had saved and made some sacrifice to have this trip. Making plans together for it had been exciting for all of them. The children are respectful to their parents and clearly appreciate being able to enjoy such a wonderful family vacation. It is the *contrast* between the children in the two cabins that has discouraged the parents in Cabin 1. They realize something is wrong.

Working together to overcome financial hardship can promote consideration for others and build protective family alliances. Wealthy families can have so many opportunities for *individual* stimulation and excitement that strong family bonds may become less important. Family members are able to do their "own thing" with little consideration for the rest of the family. This may produce children who are self-centered and have less family loyalty.

Wealth has its disadvantages. According to the Bible, wealth won't help you into heaven. Psalm 49:8–9: "For a soul is far too precious to be ransomed by mere earthly wealth. There is not enough of it in all the earth to buy eternal life for just one soul to keep it out of hell." Matthew 19:23–24: "Then Jesus said to his disciples, 'It is almost impossible for a rich man to get into the kingdom of heaven. I say it again—It is easier for a camel to go through the eye of a needle than for a rich man to enter the kingdom of heaven.'" Wealth can corrupt us and make us less responsive to God's word. When wealth permits parents to ignore God's directions in the Bible, wealth becomes a handicap to their children.

The Bible says (Luke 2:24) that after Jesus was born Joseph offered a sacrifice of two turtle doves instead of the usual sacrifice of a lamb. Mosaic law permitted this if the parents were poor. Joseph was a carpenter and Mary was not a working mother. The parents God chose for Jesus were not wealthy. I assume God felt this was to his Son's advantage.

Having money does not automatically prevent a parent from raising a mentally healthy child. There are advantages for children of parents who do not have to worry about money. One very important benefit is that the mother does not need to work, allowing her more time to protect, nurture, and influence her children. Affluence should also result in the father being more available to his family. On the other hand, these parents have attractive options such as travel, education, entertainment, housekeepers, and nannies, which make it easier for them to spend less time with their children as they pursue more *self*-satisfying activities. Wealthy parents frequently become accustomed to and demand "quality" in their life experiences. While spending so much energy in a search for the "best" life has to offer, they can become pampered and spoiled. Self-indulgent parents tend to raise self-indulgent children.

Over-indulged Children

Wealthy children may be so indulged there is little motivation for them to compete in the outside world. A nine-year-old boy was referred to me because he did not socialize. His domain was an entire wing of a mansion. He had the best VCRs, video games, computers, and toys at his fingertips. He had a tennis court, tennis coach, and a swimming pool. Why should he socialize? He did not see the point. All his needs and wishes were met at home and everything else seemed a step down. Only after extensive counseling were the parents able to limit his "toys" and provide sufficient pressure and incentives to cause him to leave his luxurious surroundings to play with other children.

When children become accustomed to having all their entertainment *provided* by their parents, they may abandon play that requires effort. They may dislike sports and other activities that require exercise. This causes them to have less in common with their classmates. Their interpersonal relationships may be affected if they exert minimal energy to make or keep friends. The parents may try to compensate by providing expensive toys to draw "friends" or by inviting other children on elaborate trips. Such children may appear happy, well liked, or even sophisticated in situations orchestrated by their parents, but they are often uncertain and immature when in less familiar and uncontrolled situations.

Affluence allows parents and children to avoid activity that is uninteresting and monotonous. These parents hire others to mow the yard, wash the car, make the bed, clean the house, wash clothes, or cook. The more wealthy they become, the more "work" can be avoided. Unfortunately for their children, the parents can also avoid much of the work of parenting. They may try to escape the work of parenting, intending to minimize "non-quality" time with their children. As a result, the *total time* spent with their children can decrease drastically. Car pools can be delegated to nannies or housekeepers. There are few family work projects or chores for wealthy children. The parents' emphasis is on providing *entertainment.* These children see their parents living a life of luxury, never appreciating that their parents obtained this luxury by effort. Affluent children may never see the strengths of their parents' personalities that permitted the parents to *become* successful and gain wealth.

Having Their Own Money

Some children have had their own bank account since birth. Through childhood and adolescence, moneys received as gifts are placed into their accounts. It is courteous and also lessens irresponsible spending if a child writes the givers of the money to thank them and tell them *how* the money will be used. Furthermore, when children have their own money, it should be clear from the onset that the parents will control how it is spent. Children often assume that having their "own" money means they can spend the money however they choose.

When children have their own money, parents sometimes permit them to buy or do something that the parents would normally not approve. For example, a parent may not want a child to have a TV in his or her room but will allow it when the child uses his or her own money. Thereafter parents may be reluctant to use grounding from TV as a punishment because it was bought with the child's own money. The same scenario occurs with VCRs, telephones, room and car stereos, pagers, and concert tickets. If the child is allowed to withdraw money impulsively and spend it foolishly, it defeats the purpose of having a savings account.

Parents are sometimes surprised to learn that the money in the account may *legally* be the child's own money. Wealthy grandparents may avoid inheritance taxes by making monetary gifts to grandchildren each year for a college fund. Under the Uniform Transfers to Minors Act, this money must be given to the child when he or she becomes an adult (depending on the individual state, this could be set at eighteen or twenty-one years of age).[1] The parents and grandparents can only *hope* the children decide to use this money for college.

Too Much Privacy

Affluent families can provide children with their own bedrooms. Having siblings share a room will invariably lead to conflict. Who can say whether this is good or bad? Learning to be civil and considerate while sharing a room with a brother or sister may provide a positive lesson for children. Children who have a bedroom to themselves can become possessive and territorial about "their" room. Parents describe how their children tell them, "Get out of *my* room!" or "Never go into *my* room without my permission." Parents have asked me how they can confront their child about marijuana they found *without* the child knowing they had been in his or her room.

Parents lose a useful deterrent when they decide not to enter a child's room. Children who know that their parents may come into their room are unlikely to hide drugs or alcohol there. Parents who regularly are in their child's room have assurance no uninvited guest is sleeping there. Room cleanliness and child study habits cannot be monitored through a closed door. When parents feel they cannot go into their children's rooms, it is a sign that privacy is being given excessive consideration.

Children Who Are Bored

Overindulged children frequently complain of *boredom.* Wealthy parents who are making freedom from boredom an important goal in *their* own lives don't want their children to be bored either, and they frantically search for new and more exciting ways to stimulate and entertain them. Parents must resist being drawn into the children's perpetual "feel good" frenzy. Technology is changing our children's interests and motivation. Television, computers, movies, amusement parks, virtual reality, video games, and special effects create a realistic *illusion* of danger, intrigue, romance, athletic prowess, and power. For children the line between what is an illusion or fantasy, and what is reality, is less clear than it is for adults. This technology is appealing to youngsters as it makes them feel strong, brave, dangerous, sexy, and smart without taking any risk or expending any effort. If the "feeling" children get is not as satisfying as expected, they may become angry and blame technology and their parents. Parents then try to pacify them by arranging more stimulating entertainment. This process gives children un-healthy power over their parents.

Children's "wants" will become increasingly more elaborate and expensive. By the time some children of indulgent parents are seniors in high school, they have owned several new cars, dined in the finest restaurants, traveled extensively abroad, been accompanied by their friends to extravagant resorts, and routinely bought themselves expensive clothes and toys. It becomes a chal-lenge for them and their parents to find something not "boring" to do. It is a sign something is *wrong* when chil-dren regularly complain they are "*bored*." Parents should be able to find constructive *tasks* or *chores* for children who complain of boredom.

When my wife and I married, blending two families, our teenage children were not excited about the modest cottage we planned to remodel for our new home. They wanted a "two story." When construction began, we made the children work with us on the weekend to clean the building site. They complained we were unfair. Soon their involvement in this family work program began to improve their attitude about our home. Over the months of construction, the complaining stopped and they began to show friends their future home with pride. Enforcing this project was not particularly fun for my wife or me. Often we felt, "Why go to this trouble?" and "This is too much work." We could have had the contractor keep the job site clean or could have hired someone to clean it. What a mistake that would have been! Most of us would like to avoid the tiresome, repetitious, difficult, and some-times unpleasant confrontations we have with our children as we teach them. We would thankfully take an easier way—if it were available. Wealthy parents *have* the resources to avoid the nitty-gritty of raising children.

The problems discussed in this chapter are not limited to the extremely rich. The negative impact of affluence is a factor in most American homes; it is a matter of degree. Many of the luxuries given to children of wealth can also be provided to children of moderate means. However, for the wealthy, "how much something costs" is not a deterrent, so parents and children are continually presented with unhealthy choices that are difficult to resist. Parents who are less wealthy just have fewer opportunities to make the same bad judgments. Even if they can afford to, parents should be careful about giving in to their child's every wish.

Useful Suggestions

- Limit the number of toys you give your child. Children who have an overabundance of toys have a greater tendency to be unappreciative and wasteful. Try to buy some toys and games that you can play *with* your children.

- Do not allow your children's birthday parties to become too elaborate. Limit the number of gifts given. Some years have your child's party *only* include immediate family and grandparents.

- Avoid regularly buying small trinkets and special treats for your child. The whining, begging power struggles that occur in grocery lines between children and their parents should motivate you to not start this habit.

- Limit the amount of time children play video games. Some parents allow children only *two*-player games in order to encourage interaction with others.

- Do not equip your child's room for entertainment. Overindulged children may have a stereo, cable television, VCR, telephone, and video games in their room. This encourages them to isolate themselves in their room, lessening involvement with parents. For such children, being "grounded to their room" has less power as a deterrent or punishment.

- Do not regularly provide a driver for your child. Driving time with children can be used to establish better communication; it may be one of the few times when child and parent have uninterrupted time together. If parents take their children to their activities, they are more aware of what their child is doing.

- Limit the use of cellular phones. Cellular phones can be a disadvantage for parent/child communication. It is common to observe parents driving and talking on the phone while their child sits ignored.

- Do not let your child have a pager. Pagers facilitate both parents and children being less accountable. With a pager, a parent may feel it is less important to control where his or her children are, because the parent can always get in touch with them. On the other hand, children are relieved they do not have to tell their parents where they are going, since parents are not able to call a specific location to check on them. The situation is tailor-made for a child to get into trouble.

- Think carefully before putting a private telephone line into your children's room. This gives parents little control over the children's use of the phone and makes enforcing a phone curfew more difficult. The result can vary from little problems, such as children not getting enough sleep because they are making or receiving late phone calls, to big problems, such as making drug contacts. I recommend that *if* a family has more than one phone line, a system be installed that has a light on the parents' phone which signals them when any phone is in use.

- A home security system should have a control panel in the master bedroom. This alerts the parents if a door or window is opened during the night. Such a system is of great help in *keeping children in,* as well as keeping burglars out.

- If you give children everything they want with no effort required of them, they may not learn there is a direct relationship between work and gain. Some teenagers truly believe what one gets depends on how much they *wish* for it. As one teenager said, "It's not fair! She got a new car when I wanted one much *more* than she did."

- Don't give children gifts that they don't have the maturity to use or appreciate. By the time some children become sixteen years old, they may have been given so much that the parents have exhausted ways to excite them. These parents may eagerly anticipate buying their child a car, sometimes the only thing for which the child has had to wait. I have seen parents buy their child a car a year before the child is legally able to drive. Is it surprising these children sometimes sneak *their* cars out?

Wealth sometimes permits parents to continue in a destructive course of child-rearing for a period longer than would occur if the parents were not wealthy. Wealthy parents are harder to "put back on track." Wealth brings power, so friends, relatives, and doctors may be hesitant to confront wealthy parents to tell them they are neglecting or mismanaging their child. Even if approached, some wealthy parents are not receptive to such criticism and dismiss it as being said from jealousy.

Wealthy parents *can* raise their children to be fine people. However, it requires parents who have the self-discipline to stay actively involved in child-rearing and not delegate parenting to others. Parents will need to exercise restraint to not overindulge their children. They should have them *earn* special purchases and activities. They must teach their children the value of hard work, even though the parents may have reached a point in their lives where they can largely avoid it.

It can be particularly helpful if wealthy parents study the Bible. 1 Timothy 6:10 says, "For the love of money is the first step toward all kinds of sin. Some people have even turned away from God because of their love for it, and as a result have pierced themselves with many sorrows." The road to being a good parent is paved by living a godly life. The Bible gives guidance that is universal and can help parents see through some of the illusions created by wealth. Attending church and Sunday school can also bring balance into the lives of affluent families. Church promotes awareness and giving to others who have less. In short, wealthy parents need to manage their children the way they would if they were not so wealthy. It is not easy to do. Ironically, some gain material wealth to do *more* for their children, only to find it causes them to do *less.*

Wealth creates many attractive but unhealthy options for parents and children. Parents may entertain their children *and* their children's friends in increasingly extravagant and permissive ways, never realizing that they may be sabotaging their own parenting efforts.

CHAPTER TEN

Sabotaging Parenting with Sleep-overs

A "sleep-over" is when a child spends the night with a friend away from home. For many families sleep-overs are regular events. A parent of a popular girl proudly told me, "During the summer we try to have *one* night a week when she is either not over at a friend's house or has someone spending the night with her." Some parents use the quantity and quality of sleep-overs to measure their child's social success. A sleep-over has become a status symbol. Children and parents alike await the phone call inviting their child to spend the night or weekend. There are parents who bring children to me for psychiatric evaluation *because* their children are not invited to sleep-overs.

On the surface sleep-overs may seem to be beneficial

for a *young* child, or certainly not harmful. They appear to be opportunities for young children to begin to safely separate from their parents and become more independent. Sleep-overs should improve children's social skills. They permit respite for the parents who want a weekend break from the responsibilities of being a parent. Some children are so mature that exposure to a different lifestyle in other homes is not damaging and may affirm their positive feelings about their own families. However, when a child is *emotionally fragile* or when the host family is *dysfunctional,* parents put their children at risk. In either case, when sleep-overs continue into a child's teenage years, parents may rue the day they started them. A high percentage of the DWIs (driving while intoxicated), MIPs (minor in possession), drug overdoses, teenage pregnancies, injuries, acts of vandalism, and deaths of teenagers happen when teenagers spend the night *away from home.* Parents would save themselves and their children a lot of grief if they *break* their child's sleep-over habit or, even better, never let it begin.

What's Wrong with Sleep-overs?

- Parents may encourage sleep-overs because they want their children to be "popular" and have fun. However, parents unknowingly may be putting too much emphasis on *entertaining* children. Children come to *expect* exciting entertainment each weekend and blame their parents if they can't have it. Worse, it can imply that to be entertained, it is best to be *away* from your parents.

- Letting children regularly stay away from home can insidiously tear down their respect for their parents. Children will not want to stay home because there is "nothing to do." It is hard to honor people who are "old-fashioned" and "boring."

- Letting children spend nights away from home interrupts the routine that families today have such difficulty establishing. Usually the host family eliminates or slackens their rules about bedtime, phone calls, and TV, as they don't want the visitor to think they and their child are not "cool." The children usually come home from a sleep-over exhausted, irritable, and exposed to activities that their parents would not have approved. Children whose parents monitor their TV shows are always eager to visit a home where there is late night access to violent and sexual movies. It becomes increasingly difficult for these children to accept and be reintegrated into the routine of their own home.

- Sleep-overs foster the idea that it is not good for a child to have time alone. Some children seldom have the opportunity to learn to entertain themselves.

- On a sleep-over young children often are permitted privileges that are beyond what is appropriate for their age. This is done because it is a "special occasion." The problem is these special occasions come every weekend and even more frequently in the summer. One example is when the host parents take their children and friends to rock concerts. Parents who do not usually permit their children to attend a rock concert will give in and let them go because they are at a sleep-over.

- There are more overt problems that can occur during a sleep-over. If there is not adequate supervision, elementary grade children may engage in sexual play. Children in this day and time often are shockingly knowledgeable about sexual acts. Sex play today may involve oral sex and other sexual activity that would have been unknown to children twenty years ago. Irate parents will discover their child has engaged in sexual activity while at a friend's home and an uproar ensues. Parents must have enough knowledge about the host parents to be confident that they are responsible people. Even this is no guarantee. Parents may invite a child for a sleep-over and then have a baby-sitter or an older sibling stay with the children, introducing another unknown and potentially dangerous factor.

- Parents who implement the child-rearing principles of the Bible are not in the majority. If children spend two days a week in homes where the lifestyle and value system is *contrary* to their own, it can undermine the other five days of parental effort. The attractiveness of a more exciting and stimulating life at a friend's house can make living a moral life of moderation seem even less appealing.

- There may be subtle differences in parenting styles that eventually can erode the children's confidence in their own parents. For example, some parents may feel it is cute to take young children out after-hours to let them wrap a house like the older kids. This is not the end of the world, but will be harmful if children are *continually* exposed to influences contrary to their parents' values.

- Parents cannot control or fully appreciate what goes on in another child's home. A fourteen-year-old boy, raised in a family that practices many of the child-rearing principles in this book, begged his parents to let him go on a sleep-over. At one o'clock in the morning the two boys were in the bedroom making prank telephone calls. The visitor, raised in a home where no guns had ever been present, playfully pointed a rifle at his friend. He pulled the trigger and his friend was killed instantly. Sleep-overs are not always harmless.

- Preoccupation with sleep-overs causes children to become *overly* invested in the importance of "friends." Friends may encourage a teenager to defy parental guidelines and discard values that parents have spent years trying to establish. If parents give their children the idea that the most important thing in life is to have friends, the children can come to feel that the opinions of their friends should take precedence over those of their parents. Without adult input, teenagers guiding other teenagers are like the blind leading the blind.

Why Do Parents Encourage Sleep-overs?

With careful screening and selection, a sleep-over may do a child no damage, particularly if the number of them is limited. However, I can see *no* saving grace for letting teenagers have a sleep-over. Teenagers want to be away from home to get away from the control and supervision of their parents. It is sometimes a ploy to deceive their parents so they will not know what the teenagers are doing. Teenagers may set up a series of false locations, making it difficult to track them. Often the parents think their child is staying at another house when in fact the teenagers are at a location where there are no parents. Parents find themselves powerless to deny teenagers a sleep-over when it has been routine since early childhood. For all the rationalizations about the value of a sleep-over in young children, *none* apply to teenagers.

Parents are so sensitive to social pressure that they may not prohibit sleep-overs because they are afraid they will be criticized by other parents. The parents themselves may have things they prefer to do and enjoy the relief from taking responsibility for their troublesome teenager. Having their child away on a sleep-over can give parents a dangerous sense of security as they falsely assume some other parent is in control. Other parents take a position that what they don't know won't hurt them, so they prefer not knowing what their child is doing.

Sleep-overs can sabotage much of the careful work parents may have done in parenting their children. It takes courage for parents to stick by their convictions and do what is right rather than what is popular or easy. I feel sleep-overs should rarely be permitted during elementary school and then only on special occasions and under controlled conditions. They should essentially *never* be allowed after a child becomes an adolescent. It is difficult to set limits on *young* children about sleep-overs; it can become almost *impossible* by the time they are *teenagers.* My advice is to simplify your lives, ration children's sleep-overs carefully, and use the limited time you have with your children protecting and guiding them. As a shepherd with his flock, you cannot watch over your children when they are not with you. The shepherd does not allow his sheep to sleep elsewhere.

Frequent sleep-overs can cause parents to have less confidence in their judgment about their children's behavior. Parents may become uncertain whether a child's behavior is the result of family interaction, a variant of normal development, or something they were exposed to when they were on a sleep-over. Such confusion most frequently occurs when children exhibit sexual behavior.

CHAPTER ELEVEN

Sexual Behavior of Children

The heroes, villains, and ordinary people described in the Bible were driven by similar passions as we experience today. Through its stories of the consequences of sexual sin, the Old and the New Testament underscore the need for people to control their sexual nature. God destroyed the cities of Sodom and Gomorrah and all the inhabitants because they were so sexually immoral (Genesis 19:1–29). David and Bathsheba (2 Samuel 11) were punished for their adultery by the death of their first child. Sexuality is a part of life, so it is not surprising it is part of the Bible.

Child Sexuality

Sexual drives exist in all of us, even in small children. It is more palatable to perceive children as sinless and asexual. This is neither biblically nor psychologically accurate. The Bible tells us man is *born* sinful. Romans 5:12 states: "When Adam sinned, sin entered the entire human race." In Galatians 5:16, Paul described our sinful nature and sexual immorality. Parents who do not understand that children are born sexual have a tendency to look for an *outside* cause to explain sexual behavior in their children.

Children are quick to pick up on an "it is not my fault" orientation. They will join their parents in blaming others for their own uncontrolled sexual impulses. Parents sometimes later discover children also blame *their* own *parents*. This could be a partial explanation why some adults falsely "remember" they were sexually abused during childhood by a parent. Looking for someone to blame for their own sexual hang-ups, and remembering no specific perpetrator, they *assume* it must have been a parent.

The sexual feelings of children are not always obvious to adults. Children may engage in sexual play or self-gratification by stimulating erotogenic areas. Both boys and girls are sometimes discovered "playing with themselves." This may be more likely to occur when children are under stress or feel neglected. For example, it may be noticed after the birth of a sibling or during a divorce. Children will be seen rubbing against adults and other children in a sensual manner. Sexual behavior may become more overt during times when children play unsupervised. Children "play doctor," showing and touching each other's genitalia. Sleep-overs and slumber parties can stimulate sexual behavior among children. Without structure, adult supervision, and guidelines, bedlam may ensue. When children get out of control, they often exhibit explicit sexual behavior.

Most of these sexual behaviors are short-lived and disappear when stress is reduced or the parents take steps to help their children control themselves. Parents must be cautious not to overreact to a child's normal evolving sexual behaviors. Being too harsh and punitive with a child can cause excessive guilt and conflict that could interfere later with healthy sexual expression of love. By example, protection, instruction, and rebuke, parents should lead their children to express sexual feelings in ways that are condoned by society and consistent with God's law. In the process, a child's *sexual morals* are established.

Harnessing Sexual Drives

The methods parents use for shaping their children's sexual drive should be similar to those used for other drives or instincts. For example, children's aggressive tendencies are controlled, modified, and shaped by parents. If parents ignore children's aggressive behavior, those children may become dangerous to others and themselves. Parents need not be overly severe or punitive. They should not tell the child he or she is going to hell. Parents should lovingly, but firmly through many repetitions, civilize their children and help them to harness their aggressiveness. Parents should teach and show their children appropriate ways to express anger. If their child bites or hits another child, parents should control and reprimand him or her. Parents should not first assume their child must have been bitten or hit by a *perpetrator*.

The same general approach can be used when confronted by a child's sexual instinct or drive. The parent should recognize that a child has pleasurable, sexual feelings that are the forerunner to adult sexuality. When children act on a sexual feeling, because of their young age their behavior may seem bizarre or perverted. Parents should limit, reprimand, or instruct their children about controlling inappropriate sexual behavior similarly as was done with their inappropriate aggressive behavior. Parents should not be harsh, abusive, or threaten children with damnation, nor should they *assume* this behavior was provoked by sexual abuse.

Understanding normal sexual development of children will help parents differentiate normal sexual behaviors from signs of sexual abuse. Failing to make this distinction can trigger a "witch hunt" for a perpetrator instead of parents accepting their responsibility to shape and influence the child's sexual behavior. It is misguided to assume your child will effortlessly grow into a mature sexual person without your assistance.

Sexual Stimulation by the Media

Mass communication spreads sexual messages to our homes. A computer with a modem can bring pornography and sexual perversion to our children at the touch of a button. Some children and adolescents are "addicted" to perverse sexual material and/or conversation carried on through computer bulletin boards. Teenagers have clandestine meetings with others whom they have met through their computer modem. One fifteen-year-old patient, unbeknownst to me or her parents, had a twenty-five-year-old man take a bus from out of state to spend a week with her. A sixteen-year-old boy working with me in psychotherapy to clarify questions about his sexual identity was discovered to have spent hundreds of dollars on computer calls to a homosexual bulletin board. The parents stopped him from keeping a scheduled meeting with an adult homosexual.

Children today are sexually stimulated and influenced by television, movies, radio, and printed materials. Few of us escape the sexual temptations of the media. Parents may try to limit their children's exposure by prohibiting them from watching shows until they are "old enough." Some *parents* enjoy voyeuristic sexual pleasures, but want to shield their children from them. Playboy and X-rated videos are hidden, usually unsuccessfully, from their children. One reason we have difficulty protecting our children from intruding sexual stimulation is that *we* accept and enjoy it ourselves.

A child's *innate* sexual nature can express itself in *overt* sexual behavior if the child is sexually stimulated. The consequences of sexually stimulating a child vary. One important factor is biologic. Some children seem to be born more sensual and sexual than others. Adults who have their own unresolved sexual hang-ups may either sexually prey on these children or be overly punitive and harsh to them. These children, in particular, should be protected, since they unknowingly can provoke sexual feelings in adults. Parents who do not actively buffer their children early-on from over-stimulating sexual influences may find that their children become "hyper-sexed." Sexual abuse of children can cause them to have over-intense, and more adult-like erotic feelings and behaviors. Teaching these children sexual restraint becomes difficult. If children have not learned self-control before adolescence, both parents and children will suffer.

Guidelines for Parents

Children's sexual feelings and thoughts usually mature in a stage-by-stage process similar to other aspects of their personality development. They will become more adult-like in their sexuality as they get older. Parents should take into account a child's changing sexuality. For example, a father may bathe his infant daughter, but never his teenager. Although this example is obvious, judging the point when he should stop bathing his daughter may not be so clear. In general, if parents have any inkling their interaction with their child is questionable, or it provokes sexual feelings in the child or themselves, it should stop. The following suggestions may be helpful, but should be tempered by common sense, taking into consideration the child's age and special circumstances:

- Do not sleep with your child. (Fear caused by a severe storm might be a special circumstance.)
- Do not bathe with your child.

- Exercise modesty when changing clothes or bathing.
- Use privacy in your own sex life, avoiding sexual activity your child can see or hear.
- Don't encourage your child to dress in a precocious or sexy style.
- Provide adequate supervision when children are playing. Don't allow long periods of time to elapse without checking on them.
- Keep magazines with nudity and explicit sexual images out of the house.
- Don't let your child watch sexually explicit TV or movies.

In this modern age, there is little need for parents to worry about sexually over-sheltering their child. No matter how protective you try to be, your child will be sexually aware, if not sophisticated. There was a time when parents needed to *lessen* their control over their children's sexual behavior. In the Victorian era, parents' punitive and overly severe prohibitions were causing their children to feel guilty and conflicted about normal sexual feelings. This sometimes led to neuroses or unhealthy sexual inhibitions when the children became adults. Today's parents face a much different problem. Usually they need to *"tighten the lid"* on their children's expression of sexual feeling. Today's youngsters, unburdened from guilt and inner conflict, more commonly are unrestrained in expressing their sexual drives.

It is the parents' responsibility to influence, control, and shape a child's sexual attitude and morals. This process is facilitated when children are able to identify with their parents' healthy, wholesome sexuality and morality. Parents need to know what is right (the Bible can help here) and then translate it to their child. Parents who govern their own lives by God's teachings will naturally interact with each other and their children in a way that supports children developing a healthy, positive attitude and behavior toward sex. However, parents should always be vigilant to protect their children. Children's immature sexual feelings, the excessive sexual stimulation in their surroundings, and their limited ability to protect themselves make them prime targets for sexual exploitation and abuse.

CHAPTER TWELVE

Sexual Abuse of Children

In 1973, the United States Congress passed The Child Abuse Prevention and Treatment Act. It required all fifty states to pass laws making it a crime not to report sexual abuse of a child and to give civil immunity from lawsuits for anyone who reported abuse. These laws have protected and/or rescued thousands of child victims. There have also been adverse consequences to this important social legislation. Releasing individuals from liability for reporting child abuse allows more accusations that have no basis in fact. Families may be torn apart by accusations that a parent or grandparent has sexually abused a child. Such an allegation may cause irreparable damage to family relationships, even if it is demonstrated to be false.

Our vigilance for signs of sexual abuse at times seems to have become a mass hysteria or paranoia. In his book,

True and False Accusations of Child Sexual Abuse,[1] Dr. Richard Gardner writes, "Divorced fathers (and even those who are not divorced) have become afraid to bathe or shower their children, or even help them when they go to the bathroom. No sane teacher will spend time alone with a girl. Scout masters on overnight hikes are sure to travel two at a time. Many nursery schools have ongoing video tapes, and no one takes a child alone to the bathroom." In this day and time, if a child makes a sexual statement or develops a behavior that might be interpreted as a sign of sexual abuse, any adult with whom the child has been alone may be suspect.

Has Your Child Been Sexually Molested?

The media's reporting and dramatization of victims of child sex abuse keep the subject never far from our minds. Changes in a child's behavior, particularly if they have a sexual component, may cause parents to worry that their child has been abused. Such behaviors include: a toilet-trained child beginning to wet, the onset of nightmares, discovery of a rash in the vaginal or rectal area, a child not wanting to visit a particular relative, a change in sleeping patterns, discovery of a child fondling himself, hearing a child make sexual comments, a child becoming afraid to sleep in his or her own room, finding a child playing sexually with another child, and almost any change in behavior that an angry separated or divorced parent notices when the child returns from a visit with the other parent.

Although children who have been sexually abused may

exhibit behaviors like those described above, these behaviors can also be a variant of normal growing up. Also, other traumas in a child's life, such as physical illness, death of a parent or sibling, moving from a home, or divorce can cause a child to regress and behave differently. For example, family violence could result in a seven-year-old boy having difficulty sleeping, losing his appetite, arguing and fighting with friends, sucking his thumb, engaging in sex play with the little girl next door, wetting the bed, and insisting on sleeping with a parent. A knowledge of normal sexual development helps parents differentiate these behaviors from sexual abuse. However, the surest and most accurate appreciation of what a particular child's sexual behavior represents is found by parents *spending time* with their children and *observing* them.

Assessment of normal sexual behavior is difficult when parents are only superficially aware of the background and character of the day-care personnel, baby-sitters, or friends who are with their children. In these situations parents cannot rule out the possibility that their child's behavior is caused by sexual abuse because the children have been in situations where it *could* have occurred.

At some point parents may turn to a mental health professional to find out if abuse actually happened. This is not without risk. If the sexual abuse has not been so overt as to leave physical or medical evidence such as vaginal or rectal injuries, semen, bruises or lacerations, diagnosing a child as having been sexually abused is not uniformly accurate. There are mental health professionals who are too quick to "uncover" and "treat" child sexual abuse. I have seen devastating effects because of misinterpretations and distortions of data by some clinicians. Children have been taken away from their families, fathers have been jailed, and mothers have been allowed no visitation with their children. There are many more examples of devastating effects caused by mental health workers' overzealous distorting of a child's comments, drawings, and behavior to fit a pre-conceived notion of the examiner.

Recently I evaluated the five-year-old son of a female attorney. The boy had developed rude, oppositional behavior toward his mother and had become physically aggressive to a dangerous extent with his three-year-old brother. In addition, the mother had discovered the boy playing with himself. She wanted her son evaluated, but asked that I videotape the sessions. In her law practice she had seen several cases where false memories of child abuse had been planted in a client's memory by therapists. She had also tried divorce cases where sexual abuse charges were used as a powerful tool in custody battles. She wanted to take no chance a mental health professional would *lead* her child to conclude he had been sexually abused. I fully understood her being so cautious.

Although there are unavoidable circumstances that expose children to sexual abuse, many sexual abuse cases could have been prevented. I have been an expert witness in child abuse cases. The most frequent request is that I determine *if* child abuse actually happened. What a sad question! How often should your children be in situations where, if they were abused, there should be a question whether it occurred? Children who have a trusting relationship with their parents will *tell* their parents about something so significant as sex abuse. Parents should not have to get a mental health professional to interpret their children's drawings or get them to demonstrate what happened by using play therapy and sexually explicit dolls. If children are too young to discuss such matters with their parents, it is *imperative* that *parents* keep their children *safe*. Parents should consider this responsibility when they decide to have children, return to work, take a vacation, go out for dinner, or get divorced. It is the *parents'* duty to be with their children to make sure they are not sexually abused or to be certain their children are cared for in a setting where the parent will have *no doubt* that their children will be protected.

Protecting Your Children from Sexual Abuse

One would think from all the information parents are exposed to about sexual abuse that they would protect their children better. Unfortunately, some parents feel *educating* the children is the best way to protect them. This is a tactic that can expose children to even greater risk. Such an approach may dissuade parents from the most effective protection children have, the parents themselves. It is foolish and dangerous for parents to feel more secure when their children have been thoroughly "educated" about the danger of sexual abuse. Teaching a child not to let someone "touch your private parts" is not adequate protection. There is no child, no matter how educated, who is a match for an adult pedophile. It is the responsibility of parents to provide protection for their children! In today's world, this is not easy, but it is the child's best hope.

I suggest parents become familiar with literature written by Kenneth Wooden on protecting children from sexual abuse. Mr. Wooden, while a co-producer for the TV news program "20/20," interviewed convicted child molesters, rapists, abductors, and murderers. It is from these "experts" on "how to sexually abuse a child" that he obtained information to write his suggestions for parents. He found the molester looks for a child whose:

- parents are in the middle of a bitter divorce.
- family has no religious affiliation.
- parents are sexually promiscuous.

Mr. Wooden found that molesters sought children from broken or unhappy homes. These children were easier to seduce because they often were starved for attention.

In the booklet, *Child Lures*,[2] Wooden gives specific warnings to parents and makes suggestions for providing protection for their children. Many of these recommendations have to do with monitoring.

- Carefully check out youth groups and summer camps before leaving your child.
- Maintain an open relationship with your children that encourages communication.
- Stress that secrets are not kept from parents and that

children should tell you of any adult who says differently.

- Be careful about having children wear name tags. A child abuser will use this to call the child's name, giving the child a false sense of security.

Mr. Wooden describes techniques that child abusers use that render a child defenseless, such as posing as (or being) an authority figure such as police, teacher, coach, or clergy. Another ploy is telling the child there is an emergency: "Your mother is sick and was taken to the hospital—come with me," or "Your house is on fire and your mother is locked out. Do you have a house key? Hurry and come with me." Molesters use pornography to seduce children because it destroys the innocence of childhood. Exposure to explicit sexual material may lead to precocious sexual behavior. Children are more vulnerable to accepting pornography if they have seen it in their home.

There is no way young children can adequately protect *themselves* from sexual abuse. Children's immature, nonspecific sexual feelings can be stimulated by suggestive sexual materials or actions by an adult. This can lead children to engage in sexual acts, even though they do not understand adult sexuality. Even if they understood or were educated about sexual matters, they do not have the discernment or strength of character to resist a seductive adult. It is up to their parents to protect them. This can be best done, particularly when they are young, by their parents being with them. If parents find it necessary to have someone else assume this responsibility, it is their *duty* to insure that their children are safe. Parenting children is an awesome responsibility. If you have children, you have made a commitment to accept the challenge.

Two parents are usually better than one in protecting children from sexual abuse. Children are vulnerable when their caretakers are multiple and varied. Increased incidence of sexual abuse can be one of the consequences of divorce.

CHAPTER THIRTEEN

Divorce and Child Custody

The Bible makes it clear that God intends marriage to be for life. In Romans 7:3, Paul writes, "When a woman marries, the law binds her to her husband as long as he is alive." In Mark 10:7–9 Jesus says, "From the very first he made man and woman to be joined together permanently in marriage; therefore a man is to leave his father and mother, and he and his wife are united so that they are no longer two, but one. And no man may separate what God has joined together." In 1 Corinthians 7:14, Paul says that even if just one of the parents is a Christian, they should not separate, since "the children might never come to know the Lord, whereas a united family, in God's plan, results in the children's salvation."

With a large percentage of marriages ending in divorce, we have moved far from God's instructions.

Many couples marry without appreciating that their vows are a *promise to God* and their unborn children, not *only* to their spouse. A vow to God is not to be taken lightly. Two parents may agree that the love between them is gone, and both feel it will be better for them if they divorced. Do they check with God to see if he agrees to release them from their commitment to him and to their children? If God is an integral part of a marriage, shouldn't he be considered in a divorce?

Raising a child alone without the observations, judgment, support, and assistance of a mate can be a painful handicap. Parents rationalize that the children will be "better off" if they are not living in a family with two unhappy parents. Although some adults seem to be more "fulfilled" after leaving a spouse, this is rarely true for their children. Most children continue to hope their parents will reconcile and their family will be together again. Parents seldom appreciate the pain children experience during a divorce. The parents' anger toward each other is felt by their children. When parents directly or indirectly devalue their ex-spouse, the child also feels the barb. They are literally one-half of the other parent.

When children live in the battle zone of a divorce, they dread occasions when their parents are together. Parents who scream, curse, slam doors, break objects, and drive recklessly when angry can terrify a child. Children may appear preoccupied, dazed, and confused as they try to shut out the pain and suffering of seeing the parents they love tear into each other. The regular exposure of a child to such conflict can erode a child's emotional health and block future personality development.

Fortunately, children are resilient and can recover from even severe parental conflict *if* it is of *brief* duration. Children can *not* withstand years of inconsistency, fear, manipulation, rage, sorrow, uncertainty, and/or violence that sometimes continues *after* parents are divorced.

Children are at the mercy of their parents' judgment and behavior. A nine-year-old boy is in the custody of his mother and stepfather. The boy's baseball team is playing its championship game on Saturday. The father comes into town with his new wife and is eager to go to the game. The two sets of parents do not have the tolerance or self-control to discuss an arrangement that will allow both to attend without incident. It is likely that if both parents and their new spouses go to the game there will be an angry scene.

For the child's sake, one of the fathers must give up his right to be at the child's baseball game. If the mother and stepfather will not compromise, then the natural father should not attend. The pleasure and benefit his son will gain from having his "real dad" in the stands is outweighed by the emotional pain the boy would feel should his two dads get into a fistfight.

Who Gets Custody?

In 1 Kings 3:17–27, Solomon ordered that a child be cut in half and equal parts given to the arguing mothers. When the biological mother offered to give the child to the other woman, he was able to identify her as the truly loving parent. Parents today often refuse to compromise their position, even if struggling with their ex-spouse is pulling the children apart emotionally.

Parents can become so determined that a child be influenced by *their* value system instead of their ex-spouse's that they may insist upon contact with the child *regardless* of the amount of conflict it creates. Sometimes attorneys recommend that divorcing parents consult a child psychiatrist. Parents and attorneys may have an unrealistic view of what can be accomplished through the use of psychiatric testimony. Both sides may find mental heath professionals who will support their position that the child should not be placed in the spouse's custody. Having experts testify with different opinions from the same data can be disconcerting, inconclusive, and expensive. A legal fight with multiple evaluations of the children, social studies, and depositions will take a toll on children. Winning a court battle often is not worth the child casualties.

The most common custody arrangement is for one parent to be designated the managing conservator (the parent who has the child most of the time), and the other the possessing conservator (the parent who has the child every other weekend). Every other week, the children are required to have dinner one weekday with the possessing conservator. Such a schedule can disrupt the structure and consistency a child needs, and it provides another opportunity for conflict between the divorced parents. Even though both parents, with this arrangement, have frequent access to their children, the parent who is not with them may call regularly to tell the children that he or she loves them. Such calls are usually unnecessary and may create anxiety for the children. Most often the need to maintain such frequent "reassuring" contact is the need of the *parent,* not of the child.

Routinely the managing conservator (I will refer to as the mother, although it may be the father) has the ultimate authority over the child. She will decide where he or she will go to school, and church, and which doctors will be used. Fathers often become enraged by such an arrangement because they find themselves with no control. Some parents, who while in a marriage seldom spent a weekend with their children, will go repeatedly to court after a divorce to obtain a few more hours.

It would be better if fathers stopped the legal haggling over the amount of *days* and *hours* they can spend with their children and instead come to an overall conclusion about *what is best* for their children and what *realistically* they can *do* about it. *If* the father *knows* the mother is damaging the children, *if* the father is *sure* he can provide a safer and more nurturing environment, *if* the father is advised by an attorney that there is some chance of success in a court battle, and *if* the father has ample funds and can afford the cost of a lengthy court battle, then he should sue for custody. *Get it over with* so the children can have the benefit of consistency and freedom from conflict during the time that remains in their childhood.

However, if the father concludes that the mother is not *overtly damaging* the children, if he cannot offer a *clearly superior* home for the children, or if he *cannot afford* it and may not win in court, then he should *accept* his plight. The father should become reconciled to his relative lack of influence over his children's lives. His *positive* impact will be *less* if having more involvement with the children causes them continued conflict. He should simply try to be the best parent he can be and enjoy his children when he has them. There will be opportunities for the father to guide his children *if* he does not wage a continuous battle against the mother. If the father is reasonable, when the mother needs a break she may *ask* the father to spend more time with the children.

Joint Custody

In my experience, joint custody with parents equally sharing responsibility for children usually is an unsatisfactory solution. If divorced parents can negotiate an arrangement that gives consideration to each of the parents' feelings and provides for the best interest of their children, then the parents are probably compatible enough to have saved their marriage. Parents who divorce each other are usually angry and distrustful of each other. It is the exception when they work in a cooperative, cordial fashion. In many instances joint custody merely provides a mechanism for continuing conflict between the parents, and recurring trauma for the children.

If joint custody is utilized, I prefer children to have longer blocks of time with each parent. One satisfactory arrangement had the children spend one school semester with one parent and the second semester with the other. In the summer each parent had an uninterrupted six weeks with the children.

Sometimes children of divorced parents cannot tell me where they will be that night. Children who are uncertain about where they will sleep, who will pick them up from school, or whether the person who takes them to scouts will be the same one to take them home, will be confused and insecure. These children have their foundation built on constantly shifting sand. They are at risk for future emotional problems. Even when joint custody with equal time for each parent seems to work well, it has a limited period of usefulness. It becomes impractical for children to frequently move from one household to another when children are older and highly involved with school activities, friends, and other interests.

Splitting Siblings

The legal system and mental health workers do their best to provide alternatives that allow *both* parents to enjoy their children and influence their personalities and values. What if no compromise can be reached and the parents doggedly persist in each having equal access even though there is continuing conflict and trauma? Sometimes I propose that "split custody" be more seriously considered. Split custody is dividing siblings between two parents. Each parent would have a child for whom he or she is the managing conservator. This suggestion frequently is resisted by parents and judges. In my opinion, if splitting the children will avoid living in conflict, it is worth a try. There are specific situations when splitting custody has a distinct advantage. For example, "splitting" can provide a troubled child the attention and resources that would be unavailable if he or she had to share the parent with other brothers and sisters.

There is no biblical writing that condemns separating siblings. Moses (Exodus) was raised separately from his siblings, yet in adulthood re-established a close relationship with his brother Aaron and his sister Miriam. God instructed that Isaac and his half-brother Ishmael be separated and raised separately (Genesis 21:9–14). If splitting children can protect them from parental warfare, then parents, professionals, and judges should be more open to the concept. From my experience, the abhorrence of splitting siblings is not justified. Sometimes there is a good reason for them to be separated.

The Friendly Divorce

There are families who manage a divorce with less difficulty than has been described. Such exceptional parents are able to maintain a respectful, cooperative relationship with each other. They regularly communicate to ensure that rules and values for their children remain consistent. Privileges, discipline, and responsibilities are enforced equally at both homes. They will not use their children to deliver messages to each other, but communicate directly, preventing the child from distorting or manipulating. Such parents never belittle or undermine their ex-spouse to their children. The parents do not vie for the approval of their children, causing the children to become entitled, manipulative, and/or out of control.

These parents are flexible in altering visitation patterns to accommodate the needs of both families. Each is satisfied with the other's financial contributions. They agree on or accept the other's choice of schools, church, camp, and doctors. These parents exchange children from one family to the other in a cordial and helpful manner. Parents who can conduct themselves with the self-control and consideration described above may permit their children to survive a divorce emotionally unscathed. Parents still must tackle raising their children alone, something that was designed to be a two-parent job. This can be done, but it will require exceptional skill, self-sacrifice, energy, courage, and divine help.

Providing a secure base for children while they grow into adulthood is essential. Parents must continually judge the degree of responsibility their children can safely assume. Because divorced parents' time with their children may not be continuous or consistent, making correct judgments about their children and providing needed control are more difficult, particularly if the parents undermine each other's efforts. Battling an angry ex-mate *and* a rebellious youngster can make parenting almost impossible. In these complex and difficult situations, psychiatric consultation can be helpful, but a miracle may be required. A good place to look for one is in the Bible.

Divorced parents who have successfully shepherded their children through adolescence and out of high school may have made heroic efforts and sacrifices. These parents are tired and *ready* to turn over the responsibility for their teenager to a college. This may be wishful thinking. Sometimes there seems to be "no rest for the weary." Parenting is not always over when children leave for college.

CHAPTER FOURTEEN

Sending Your Child to College

Nowhere in the Bible does it say there are stages of our lives that are exempt from God's law. Somehow we have gotten the mistaken idea that colleges are "free" from God's scrutiny and influence. It is as if we have said to our children, "Sow your wild oats while you are in college. Soon you will be in the real world and have responsibilities. You are only young once. Enjoy it. God can't see you." There can be serious repercussions to sending children to college with the idea they are hidden from God. Not only can children be called to judgment unprepared (college students *are* uniquely susceptible to sudden death through automobile accidents and violence), but they become more susceptible to immoral and harmful influence when they wander from God's path.

College May Not Be Safe

Parents dream of college as a place where their children can evolve from adolescence to adulthood. They assume or hope college will buffer them from the dangers of the adult world. They have a vague notion college will provide structure, supervision, and guidance. In reality, colleges are seldom a safe haven for children. There are no curfews, no signing out of the dormitories, and no regulation of overnight guests. Lack of supervision, easy access to alcohol and drugs, and plenty of free time create an opportune climate for sexual permissiveness for the young student.

Parents should not count on college professors to provide positive influence and guidance. A college freshman said the topic the English professor gave for their class paper was, "If a pornography film featured a woman sticking needles in men's testicles, would it be a box office success? Why?" The risks for teenagers, which preoccupied parents during their children's high school years, do not disappear when they enter college; they sometimes become worse.

Going to college will change the parent/child relationship. There is no way parents can, or should, treat their college-age children the way they did when the children lived at home. However, if parents want their children to maintain a value system similar to the one they had before college, the parents need to tell them what they expect. The parents should *verbalize* what they expect of their college student in regard to use of alcohol and drugs, sexual promiscuity, study time, and church attendance. Teenagers are very concrete in their thinking. If not told, many conclude the parents are covertly giving him or her permission to disregard the rules the parents had when the child lived at home. Parents may need to continue to shoulder some responsibility for their college-age child's behavior, safety, morality, and religious life. The sound biblical principles used in guiding children through high school *still* have a place as children move into the extended adolescence of college. It is helpful if young students have the continued positive influence of their parents to bolster them.

Why do we put our heads in the sand and turn our backs on our children just because they go to college? One common reason is that parents are tired of the hassle and responsibility of raising children and feel they deserve a rest. I have seen few parents exhibit the "empty nest" syndrome (parents becoming depressed when their children leave home). Most parents are *ready* for their children to be out of the home and for them to make their own decisions. Unfortunately, letting many college freshmen decide if they will study, drink, use drugs, get enough sleep, eat healthy foods, be sexually active, go to class, and attend church is similar to leaving elementary students unsupervised in a candy store and telling them to decide what they want to eat. Parents may have a false sense of security that their children are okay when they do not know what those children are doing. Sometimes this is a dangerous delusion.

Some parents early in their child's life permitted nannies, teachers, television, and social pressure to be primarily responsible for child-rearing. It is not surprising that these parents are also quick to give college the responsibility of "finishing" their children. Strangely, other parents may not feel they have a "right" to make demands on their children once they leave for college. A closer look at this interaction will reveal that this is not a new pattern between parent and child. Usually long before their children's college stage these parents had given up much of their power to their children. An example is that of the timid parents who are afraid to go into their child's room because the child will accuse them of "invading his or her privacy." Parents who have so little power and respect from their children will have limited influence on how their children conduct themselves in college.

Partying

When parents send their children to college, they may over-emphasize the importance of children "having a good time." Social life is often presented as the focal point of the student's life. Parents may encourage their children to join fraternities and sororities without knowing whether the group's behavior contradicts the values the parents have taught. Parents hear of drunken escapades and wild parties, then joke with their children about their hangovers. We may dismiss such behavior as harmless, saying that we ourselves had similar experiences and survived them. Such an attitude does not offer adequate protection for our children.

Today's environment is more perilous. Drugs are readily available to augment or replace alcohol. Students now talk of their "drug of choice" that includes alcohol, marijuana, cocaine, speed, or hallucinogens. The moral fiber of our adolescents is weakened. Aggressive and sexual behavior is less controlled. What once was drunken revelry now becomes costly vandalism; what used to end in a bloody nose now may result in a fatal beating, stabbing, shooting, or gang assault; what in days past may have ended with a slap can now become date or gang rape; and what once was a worry about "reputation" has progressed to the impact of having an abortion, herpes, or HIV.

Study Requirements

Parents often make great sacrifices to send a child to college. Is it unreasonable to tell your college students you are sending them to college on the condition they attend class or sleep each night in the dorm or apartment you provide for them? Is it harsh to tell them you expect they will be sober and that drunken escapades are unacceptable? Are parents out of line to call their child on Saturday morning to check on whether he or she is hung-over or even came in the night before?

Students should understand that although "partying" in college may be intense and seem to be the "norm," they must achieve good grades or they may find themselves no more employable than if they had not attended college. A greater number of high school students are going to college. A college degree is no longer assurance that a graduate will find a job. Criteria that employers use to select graduating college students for jobs have become more standardized. Objective criteria, such as high grades and test scores, are used for comparing students. Businesses will only interview students who maintain a high grade point average. Whom you know and what fraternity you are in have become much less relevant. If college students are not academically competitive, parents might assist, pressure, or warn them to become better motivated and self-disciplined, or withdraw them from college until they are more mature. Spending four years accumulating a low grade point average can be a liability that is difficult to overcome.

Is it realistic to send children to college without conditions and requirements? Where will they ever find a situation where they are given lodging, board, an automobile, gas, car insurance, spending money, a country club (fraternity), and education with the only stated expectation that they "make the most of the opportunity." The irresponsible lifestyle some parents provide for college students may make it difficult for them and the *parents* when their children try to adjust to the "real world" once they leave college.

It might be useful for parent and child to view college like a job. Would it be unreasonable for a parent to require the student to work (class + study time) a seven hour day? Try this calculation: Divide the expense of a semester of college by the number of hours your student is *in class* or *studying*. It might surprise you how much you are "paying" your child. Many college freshmen could *still* benefit from a parent's advice about study time. The recommended college load (fifteen hours) is only three hours in class a day. Students coming from packed days of class and extracurricular activities in high school often are bewildered by the amount of free time they have in college and may drift aimlessly. Giving a college freshman a study schedule may be helpful.

Requiring Church Attendance

Does your college student go to church? I have four natural children and two stepchildren who have gone to college. I have looked at more college dormitories, found more off-campus apartments, and attended more fraternity and sorority homecoming brunches on more college campuses than most fathers. It is embarrassing to admit that until the senior year of our last college child, I had never attended a church service where any one of our children was in college. When we looked for college housing, we never even tried to locate the most convenient and appropriate church for our children to attend. We unintentionally conveyed the clear message to them that attending church was so unimportant that it wasn't even worth *mentioning.*

Some parents say college is an opportunity for their children to sort out their true feelings about religion and to make *their own choice.* When a child is nursing a hangover on Sunday morning, it is not a deep, philosophical religious struggle keeping him or her from going to church. If children want to ponder the merits of religion, what is wrong with them doing it on their own time *after* they are not supported by parents? I feel obligatory church attendance is the most innocuous, but possibly

143

the most helpful, condition parents could make on their college-bound child. Can you imagine the positive effect on college students if they went to church every Sunday morning? For one thing, it would influence how late they stayed out and what they did on Saturday night. This in itself might save their lives.

Parents may argue that such an approach is not practical. Recently, a father who heard me comment about making church attendance a requirement for going to college asked, "How can you know whether they attend? Aren't you setting up a rule you cannot enforce?" It is true that if children have been raised without religious influence, it will be difficult to *make* them go to church when they are at college. On the other hand, the father's question demonstrates how ready parents are to give up the little control they have. Although some might consider it *unreasonable,* it certainly is within the parents' *power* to *not* send their children to college *unless* they go to church. Parents sometimes say they "cannot" when actually they mean they "will not."

If parents *decide* church attendance is required at college, one strategy for checking compliance might be setting a routine of the parents calling the child each Sunday after the *parents* return from church. Parents and child could compare and discuss their respective sermons. This is not cruel and unusual punishment! Parents may be surprised that it improves communication. College students sometimes are difficult to engage in conversation. Questions such as "What have you been doing? How are your classes? What did you do last night?" are regarded by the student as inane and nosy. It may be a relief to both of you to be able to talk about religion. Another positive strategy is to periodically make a college visit and accompany your children to their church.

What should parents do if their college child regularly defies them? Well, it is *too late* to use the rod! If the parent has provided clear, realistic expectations and conditions for going to college and the child regularly does not meet them, the parent should *stop paying* for college. This is not a profound or novel suggestion. Three thousand years ago, Solomon (Proverbs 17:16) said it was a waste to pay for the schooling of a student who had no intention of learning. If students understand that irresponsible conduct and insufficient study time could cause their parents to stop paying for their college education, it should cause them to improve their performance.

The degree of parental involvement a college student will need depends on the maturity of the teen and the college he or she attends. Some parents recognize their children's need for a more structured setting by directing them to colleges where student activity is better regulated. The point is that some parental control and influence is possible, if parents decide to try. There is nothing wrong with parents continuing to act like parents if their dependent student continues to act like a child. When children enter college, the parents' responsibility for their children's behavior is largely completed, but it is not over. College children will not need the intensity of parental involvement they required in high school, but most will need some guidance.

A Parent/Student Contract

There are parents who practice what I am preaching. The following is an actual copy of the rules parents gave their son when he entered Baylor University:

Rule and Words of Wisdom for Our Son Marc Bonham Magness

From your loving parents

1. Your education at college is far more important than any girl or fraternity.
2. It is better to fail on an exam than to cheat on it and pass.
3. Conduct yourself on every date and social function as if your mother and God were right beside you. Actually your mother isn't, but God is!
4. You may not get married while you are in college.
5. Always be kind and considerate of others, especially your roommates.
6. Do not procrastinate, especially when it involves homework.
7. An average grade is one that is not good enough.
8. On Sundays you must attend church or Sunday school unless you are ill.
9. Remember, no problem is too great for God to handle, no sin too great to be forgiven.
10. Your parents are the next best thing to God on earth. They love you deeply and want only the best in life for you.

11. Your parents are forgiving.
12. Last but not least, if you follow all the above advice, but forget your relationship with God through Jesus Christ, then nothing else really matters.

Sending a child to college with such clear biblical guidance seems a uniquely loving act.

When college students come home for vacation it will, of course, disrupt the peace and quiet that the empty-nesters have grown to savor. However, parents need not adjust their schedule to a college lifestyle while their children are home. College students should reintegrate themselves to their families' routines. Parents should expect their children to eat some meals with the family, to come home at a reasonable hour, not to trash their rooms, and to attend church with the family. Parents should not tolerate behavior that is inconsiderate, a bad influence on siblings, immoral, or disrespectful. For college-age children, home need not be as much fun as being on their own. If it is, children may *never* decide to leave home.

Raising a child is like running through a dangerous obstacle course. Parents may successfully negotiate most of the hurdles of child rearing only to watch their child falter because they stop parenting before the child has reached his or her finish line. Parental influence should continue when children go to college, but parents can no longer be their children's shepherd. Cutting these apron strings may lead parents to more fervent prayer.

CHAPTER FIFTEEN

Prayer and Parenting

Great men in the Bible, such as Abraham, Joseph, Moses, David, Jesus' disciples, Paul, and Jesus himself, were all fervent in prayer. In Paul's letter to Timothy (1 Timothy 2:1), he listed in his "instructions on worship" that *first* there be prayer.

This chapter on "Prayer" is put at the end, rather than the beginning, of this book because of how the book evolved. Only *since* reading the Bible and writing this book have I appreciated the great value prayer can have in rearing children. I now recognize that parents who have strong faith seem "different" from other parents. They appear more secure and hopeful when facing a difficult personal crisis.

Paul says in Galatians 5:22, "When the Holy Spirit controls our lives he will produce this kind of fruit in us:

love, joy, peace, patience, kindness, goodness, faithfulness, gentleness, and self-control." The Holy Spirit does not promise we will be rich, handsome, strong, forever young, or forever well. A strong faith may not always protect a child from emotional illness. However, it is much easier for a psychiatrist to identify and treat children's problems if they live in a family where parents have gifts such as love, patience, and self-control.

For a believer, prayer is an indispensable part of life. Many parents regularly pray for their children. These parents believe that their faith and personal relationship with God through prayer give them the wisdom and strength to guide and protect their children. I have observed the positive impact of parents' prayers on child-rearing.

Earlier in this book, the power of children's identification with their parents was stressed. If parents spend time with their children, the children will take on many of the parents' characteristics and values. This is an awesome responsibility for a parent. How do you want your children to remember you, and what behaviors would you like your children to emulate? I believe that in the process of prayer we may be at our *best* as role models for our children. Thanking God for his protection and gifts, admitting our own shortcomings, seeking forgiveness and assistance to live according to God's will, and asking help for others in need project a powerful, benevolent example for our children.

When parents arrange opportunities for family prayer, they will *automatically* place their family in a wholesome, healthy environment. When you are praying, it is more likely you are sitting together at the dinner table or at a church picnic rather than in the neighborhood bar. The act of prayer, even without strong conviction that God will answer, places families in more positive life situations.

Although people more commonly pray in silence, "one on one" with God, some praying should include the whole family. How are our children to learn how to pray? There are situations where family prayer seems to come naturally. These times include children saying their prayers with parents at bedtime, having a blessing with meals, praying in unison at church, and participating in family devotion or Bible study.

Prayer at Bedtime

If parents did not grow up in a family where prayer was routine, they may feel self-conscious when praying with their children. At first it may feel unnatural or insincere. Praying, like most actions, gets more comfortable the more often we do it. It is easier if we start praying with our children when they are young. Tucking children into bed and helping them say their prayers is true "quality time" for parent and child. Bedtime prayer is also a way for *parents* to practice and become more comfortable praying. An innocent and trusting child provides a model for parents on how God wants us to approach him. In Matthew 18:3–4, Jesus told his disciples, "Unless you turn to God from your sins and become as little children, you will never get into the kingdom of heaven. Therefore anyone who humbles himself like this little child is the greatest in the kingdom of heaven." Bedtime prayer with a child may be a parent's first step in making prayer a regular part of family life. It can begin a lifelong habit of prayer for both parent and child.

Prayer at Mealtime

Another natural, comfortable time for parents to pray is at dinner. Prayer at mealtime can be a springboard to improved communication in the family, and may identify specific needs of family members. Some families claim they are too busy to eat dinner together. They may argue that their schedules are different and each wants to go his or her individual way. How can children, who have not yet become mature and competent individuals, go their own way? Children need loving, wise, protective parental guidance. One place children receive such guidance is at dinner with their family, particularly when it begins with prayer

The family dinner, a tradition for centuries, appears headed for oblivion. Today's high-tech, hectic lifestyle has made family dinner no longer routine. The older the children, the harder it is to have them regularly at dinner with the family. Social, work, school, and athletic activities are given a higher priority. Getting the family together at mealtime requires determination, planning, and self-sacrifice. It is well worth the effort! Most families find having dinner together warm and comfortable as family members share experiences and plan upcoming activities. However, some families view eating dinner together as an unpleasant, if not dreaded, experience.

Praying before meals can help defuse angry, bitter, mean-spirited communication.

During my group therapy with children, a snack is served. The children in the group often perceive it as being like a family. I am the "father," there is a female co-therapist, the "mother," and the children in the group see themselves as the "brothers" and "sisters." The group therapy allows more accurate diagnosis of the problems the children are having at home. Sadly, it may also give some children something they seldom received during childhood—a regular meal with their "parents."

Parents should realize that if there is a problem having mealtime with their children, *there is a problem.* The solution is *not* to *avoid* mealtime. Family meals are an excellent barometer for judging how family members feel about each other. It is a good place to recognize and resolve minor conflicts before they become major problems. *Add prayer,* and parents will be stacking the deck in favor of their children's good mental health.

Prayer at Church

If a parent wants to learn to pray, what easier way than to attend church? There the congregation is coached in praying technique by listening to the minister, reading from prayer books, and being led by church leaders. When children accompany their parents to church, they will identify with their parents as the parents demonstrate their beliefs and values in prayer. Is this not the example we want to be to our children? Where are we better? Church gives parents direction and support in establishing moral and ethical values for their children. It places both parent and child with others who have similar beliefs and demonstrates the benefit of having lives that are shaped by the word of God. Regular attendance at church proves to children that their parents feel going to church and living godly lives are important.

I often hear parents say they want their children to have different ("better") friends. Parents may conclude that the best place to look for these "better" friends is in a church. However, teenagers may be too afraid of rejection to try to make new friends in a church they did not grow up in. Sometimes their fears may be justified. Some teenagers, even Christian ones, are not eager to add new friends to their "group." If you want your children to have friends who have "church values," get them to church early in their lives. And if the church in your neighborhood doesn't fit you, "shop around." Choose a church whose leaders and members project a lifestyle you admire and believe to be godly.

Taking children to church is the parents' responsibility. Few children prefer to attend church, rather than sleep late or watch TV. Children are not capable of deciding whether organized religion and church attendance are useful to them. Not attending church is one way teenagers assert their independence. Parents may give in to their resistance to go to church, rationalizing that this is a normal developmental step for the teenager and that they are just "growing up." True, it is important that teenagers begin to make their own decisions and become more independent from their parents. However, there are thousands of opportunities for them to do this without allowing them to withdraw from the positive influence of regular church attendance. Parents can loosen their ties to their children in many ways. Church attendance is one place where parents should stand their ground!

As children go through adolescence, their own parents' seem old-fashioned and oppressive, but other adults may seem "cool" and can become role models and/or mentors. Although not all people in church are good, church is one of the best places I know to find other adults who can be a positive influence for your children. Church can be a protective, stabilizing, guiding support system for parents and children. When a parent is learning to pray, a good place to start might be, "Please God, keep my child under the protection and influence of a church."

Family Devotion

Another occasion for family prayer is family devotion. Prepared lessons designed for regular family devotions are available through most churches. These family discussion times may focus on values, behaviors, and family relationships, and will begin and/or end with prayer. For parents who seldom pray in the home, who infrequently attend church, and whose friends are not religious, having family devotions may seem unrealistic.

Some parents are more comfortable using family "meetings" to improve communication, work out family conflicts, and plan family activities. From my point of view, either the "family meeting" or "family devotions" could be very useful. Although both can accomplish the same psychological purpose, family devotions offer one more way for the parents to demonstrate to their children that God and his teachings are important. Commonly, when an emotionally disturbed child is evaluated by a psychiatrist, a problem in family communication and family interaction is discovered. Family therapy may be recommended. Having a psychiatrist help a family communicate and work out family conflicts in family therapy can feel *more* awkward and uncomfortable than family devotions, and certainly is more expensive.

Some parents first turn to prayer when faced with a family crisis. Although prayer may calm a vicious divorce or provide direction for a troubled child, these painful life situations might never have occurred if prayer had always been a part of the family's life.

The result of parents' prayer is seldom immediate. Its effect may not be fully appreciated until the children are almost grown. Putting children to bed with prayer, having children together for dinner with a blessing, praying with children during regular church attendance, and praying at a weekly family devotion quietly but steadily shape children and parents into what God wants them to become.

SUMMING UP

Principles for Child-Rearing:

- *Worship God.* A strong spiritual life will lead to a loving and effective family life.

- *Marry for life.* Parenting is meant to be a two-person job.

- The most effective way to influence your children is to *spend time with them* and *be a good example.*

- *"Honor your father and mother."* This is the basis for children developing respect for authority.

- *Discipline* is part of love. Do *not* permit your children to be *defiant.*

- Establish a *routine* for your children's *bedtime, eating habits,* and *personal hygiene* before they are six years old.

- Teach your children they are important because *God loves* them; confidence and self-esteem will follow.

- A parent's *love,* like God's, should be *forgiving,* but there should be *consequences* for bad behavior.

- More *"quality time"* with children should not cause the *"quantity"* of time to decrease.

- *Limit sleep-overs* to special occasions.

- Seek opportunities for you and your children to *pray together.*

- Raise your children in an environment where they will have other positive role models. Participate in church activities.

- Make meals together a family routine and carefully protect this time.

- Teaching your children to "make the right choices" is no substitute for *parental judgment and protection.* Children can understand danger *before* they have the maturity and self-control to avoid it.

- Know your children, their friends, and their activities well enough to judge *when to protect, and when to let go.*

- Make *home* a secure "*base*" for your children, but also *prepare* them to safely *move out* into the adult world.

- *Wealth* creates special challenges in being an effective parent. Wealthy parents must *not delegate* the work of parenting.

- *Require,* as one condition for sending children to college, that they regularly *attend church.*

If your goal is to raise children the way God would like, study God's parenting manual, *the Holy Bible.*

Postscript

Ten years after Ann Lawson's death, I wrote her husband the following letter:

Dear Ray,

Hope that you are doing well. I am sorry it's been so long since we've gotten together. You know I've remarried. I now have two stepdaughters and little Dan is living with us.

I am writing mainly to ask a favor of you. Some uncharacteristic things have been happening to me since Ann's death. I have stopped drinking, only occasionally smoke a cigar, and haven't been to Las Vegas for a year and one half. I have started to go to church regularly, now say a blessing with meals, give money to the church, and recently a friend asked me to join a Bible study group. *Please,* if you still have any influence with Ann, call her off of me. I am about as good as I can stand! I am very satisfied with my life and being a child psychiatrist. I do not want to become a preacher!

Warm regards,
Dan

Two weeks later I received a Bible for Christmas and began writing this book. Ann wasn't through with me yet.

NOTES TO MY CHILDREN—a place for recording family traditions, child-rearing experiences, and personal notes.

_____

_____

_____

_____

_____

_____

_____

_____

_____

_____

_____

_____

_____

_____

NOTES

INTRODUCTION

1. The Authorized King James Version of the Bible is used for counting pages.

CHAPTER FOUR

1. "The Effects of Mother-Child Separation: A Follow-Up Study," *British Journal of Medical Psychology,* 29:211, 1956.

2. "The Nature of Love," *American Psychologist,* 13:673, 1958.

3. "Hospitalism: An Inquiry into the Genesis of Psychiatric Conditions in Early Childhood," in R.S. Eisler et al. (eds.), *The Psychoanalytic Study of the Child,* International Universities Press, vol. 1, pp. 53–74, New York, 1945.

CHAPTER FIVE

1. William G. Golding, *Lord of the Flies,* Aeonian Press, 1975.

CHAPTER SEVEN

1. Dr. James Dobson, *The New Dare to Discipline,* Tyndal House Publishers, Inc., 1990.

CHAPTER NINE

1. Reference: Ron Cresswell, attorney, Locke Purnell Rain Harrell, Dallas, Texas.

CHAPTER TWELVE

1. Richard A. Gardner, *True and False Accusations of Child Sex Abuse,* Creative Therapeutics, 1992.
2. Kenneth Wooden, *Child Lures: The Power of Positive Prevention,* The Wooden Publishing House, 1986.